Dream Catchers

HOMEMADE MOBILES, WALL HANGINGS, AND JEWELRY

CHARLINE FABREGUES
(MARCEL MÉDUSE)

SCHIFFER PUBLISHING
4880 Lower Valley Road • Atglen, PA 19310

CONTENTS

ACKNOWLEDGMENTS 4
FOREWORD 5
INTRODUCTION 6

JUNGLE
DREAM CATCHER 8

BUFFALO
DREAM CATCHER 12

ALL-WOOL
DREAM CATCHER 17

PAPER FEATHER
DREAM CATCHER 22

FLOWERY
DREAM CATCHER 26

AMERINDIAN
DREAM CATCHER 30

- SOPHISTICATED DREAM CATCHER 36
- TRIPLE-WEAVE DREAM CATCHER 40
- ROMANTIQUE WALL HANGING 45
- MARINE WALL HANGING 50
- PRIMITIVE WALL HANGING 54
- SUCCULENT WALL HANGING 59
- POM-POM MOBILE 64
- LUCKY EARRINGS 68
- WOVEN NECKLACE 71
- LUCKY NECKLACE 76

ACKNOWLEDGMENTS

Writing these lines is particularly moving.... I've always loved books, and having the opportunity of writing one has been a fantastic experience for me. I hope that this book gives you as much pleasure reading it, discovering new things, and experimenting as it gave me writing it!

I would like to express all my love and gratitude to my "Marcel," my man, for his unconditional support; for the hours he spent helping me with cutting out, sanding down, drilling, and gluing without (or almost without) complaint; for his confidence in me; for his patience; and for everything else he has brought me every day for ten years now...

To my son, my little boy, my pride, and my love.... When he was just three years old, he whispered the name "Marcel Méduse" in my ear. Without him, I wouldn't be here today.

To my parents for their immense love.

A huge thank you to my friends, my soul sisters, and everyday supporters! To you, Val, who always has great ideas, who opened your house and your heart to me, who posed patiently for my photos, and who has always encouraged me.... To you, Letisse, for your precious help, your support, your smile, your confidence, and your useful scissors.... To our silly jokes and uproarious laughter, our endless cups of coffee, our shopping sprees! I hope we grow old together in love and laughter!

To you, Nadege, for having believed in me, for being there for me, and for everything you have given me over the years....

To Juliette, my editor, for having proposed this project, for having believed in me and encouraged me, and for supporting me and giving me excellent advice!

My heartfelt thanks to my partners "Perles & Co," "Créavéa," "Matière Première," and "Couture & Co" for their confidence, the exchange of ideas, and their advice!

And to you! Together or individually.... For the super encounters either real or virtual, for your messages, your words, and the wonderful things you have brought me! It's also thanks to you that I have been able to live my dream for nearly three years now....

CHARLINE FABREGUES

FOREWORD

Fascinated by the Bohemian chic universe and driven by her desire for serenity, relaxation, and naturalness, Charline has been creating dream catchers—inherited from Amerindian tradition—for several years. Numerous legends, unique to each tribe, circulate around this object. With the delicacy of a spider's web, it traps bad dreams in its weave and lets good dreams filter through and slide along its feathers to the sleeper. Full of strong symbolic values, it's a key object of Amerindian culture and has an almost mystical dimension.

Dream catchers have become a popular item in decoration, mainly for children, but they remain highly symbolic. The care taken in their creation and attention paid to small details is very important for Charline. Fascinated by working with different materials and joining components with different textures, she makes unique models from natural elements, lace, ribbons, and beads. She adds personal touches, such as origami-made butterflies, leather feathers, and small pendants that she designs and makes herself.

During a walk along the beach she fell in love with driftwood, which awoke a burning desire to work with it: smooth, knotty, twisted—she finds it sublime! It also opened the doors to another facet of her creativity.

Charline's dream catchers are therefore all completely unique, each expressing her state of mind while she worked on it.

In 2014, Charline created her own brand, Marcel Méduse (a lovely name her small son whispered in her ear) to develop her craft and to share her models with a larger public. Today, she has chosen to make her living out of her passion and dedicate herself entirely to her art. She set up a workshop in her home and makes each piece with the same desire and love of work well done.

INTRODUCTION

Making a dream catcher isn't particularly complex, but you need to have good materials and also know certain basic techniques. It requires patience and precision, which, once you have acquired the necessary dexterity, will give you a great deal of pleasure and satisfaction. The creative possibilities are endless, so give your imagination free rein!

Materials used:

- **Embroidery hoop:** This is made up of two wooden or plastic circles that fit one into the other. The outer circle has a screw that tightens the hoop around the cloth. For your creations, a wooden hoop is better from an esthetic point of view. Normally used for embroidery, you can give it another use as the base of your creation!

- **Lampshade hoop or the skeleton of a lampshade:** These are metal circles initially intended for making your own lampshade, and they come in different sizes. They can also be used as the base of your creations.

- **Hot glue gun:** This is an electric tool that melts and applies batons of thermo-fusible glue. Be careful: the glue coming out of the gun is very hot! Avoid touching it or you'll get a nasty burn! This highly practical tool is indispensable for nearly all creative activities.

- **Punch pliers:** This is a mechanical tool used for piercing or punching cloth or leather. It's useful for piercing textile feathers before threading them.

- **Cutting pliers:** These small, steel pliers are useful for cutting the ends of feathers and small metal pieces.

- **Long-nose pliers:** Mainly used in jewelry, these pliers (often used in pairs) will enable you to hold and open the split rings you'll use to attach pendants, pom-poms, or beads to your creations.

- **Dressmaker's scissors:** These scissors are very sharp and are indispensable for cutting cloth and leather. They shouldn't be used for cutting anything else (paper for example) to avoid blunting them. You should keep an ordinary pair handy for cutting out patterns, etc.

- **Cotton thread:** A very strong thread for tying driftwood to your embroidery hoops and also for hanging up your work once it's finished.

- **Nylon thread or fishing twine:** This strong, transparent thread will add an airy feel to your creations, allowing you to suspend them without the fastening line showing.

- **Jade thread:** This is strong, supple polyester thread often used for pearl necklaces. It is useful for hanging items from your dream catchers or wall hangings you thread beads onto.

- **Satin ribbons in various widths, rickrack trim, Lurex thread, etc.:** These haberdashery accessories will be used to decorate and dress your dream catchers and give them volume and texture.

- **Big-eye beading needle:** This is a large, supple needle with a central eye. It will make the task of threading beads onto the Jade thread so much easier. Pass the thread through the central eye and slip your beads one by one onto the needle... simple!

- **Natural or synthetic feathers:** These are one of the basic elements in dream catchers. Don't hesitate to choose lovely, good-quality feathers: they will add softness and character to your creation. Feathers have their own particular characteristics... for example, eagle feathers represent courage, and owl feathers represent wisdom.

- **Wooden, resin, plastic, and glass beads:** Big, small, round, flat, with patterns or natural, they add a precious touch to your creation. They also keep feathers in place on the thread.

Different dream catcher centers explained in this book:

- **Woven center:** This is the original and traditional technique for dream catchers. It forms a shape similar to a spider's web, which will imprison bad dreams. Weaving, done using Jade thread, for example, takes some time and can take several forms, from the most traditional to the most modern (explained in this book).

- **Lace center:** Lace, crocheted using fine cotton thread, is close to traditional weaving. It has the look of a spider's web where bad dreams are caught while adding a soft and romantic dimension to your creation. You can use a doily or, for the more creative, crochet your lace yourself. Your piece will be even more unique and precious!

- **Driftwood center:** Driftwood is a natural material found on the beach above the high-tide mark. It is wood that, after several weeks, months, or years in salty water, is polished, hollowed, and shaped by salt, wind, waves, and tides. Driftwood doesn't need any chemical treatment because it is naturally protected by its high salt content.

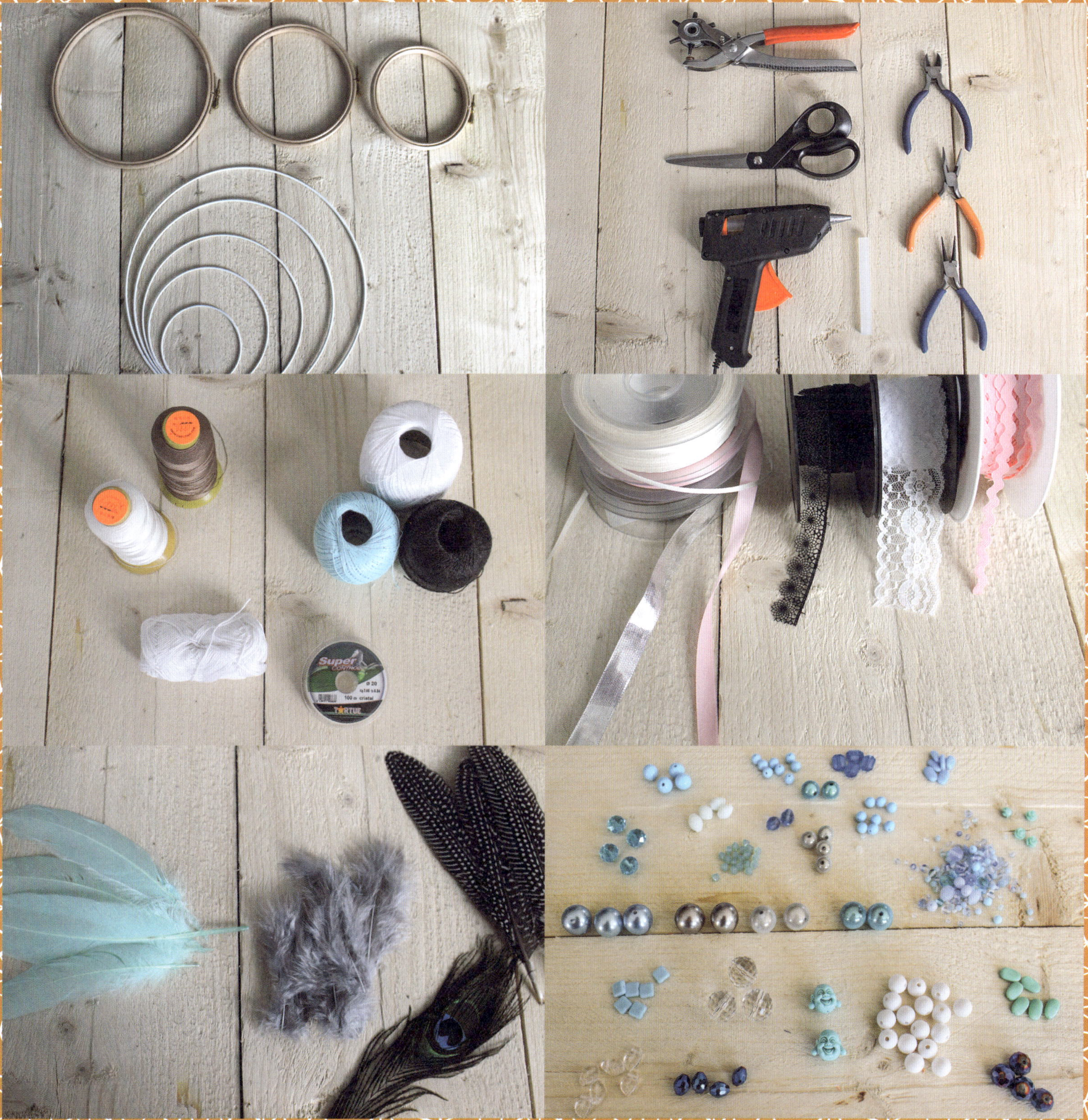
Super
TORTUE

Materials

- 1 embroidery hoop 9 7/16 in. (24 cm) diameter
- Small toy animals
- 1 piece of driftwood
- Cotton thread
- Jade thread
- Natural feathers in brown tones (guinea-fowl or peacock feathers)
- Smooth feathers in green tones
- Unpolished and polished wooden beads 11/16 in. (18 mm)
- 1 tagua nut (vegetable ivory) 1 3/8–2 in. (35-50 mm), aniseed color
- Miracle beads in gold, green, and olive green 5/16 in. (8 mm)
- Miracle beads in gold, green, and olive green 11/16 in. (18 mm)
- Round snakeskin beads
- 2 tagua discs in lime and grey 11/16 in. (18 mm)
- Glitter ribbons in green and brown tones
- Satin ribbons in green and aniseed tones 1/8 in. (3 mm), 1/4 in. (6 mm), and 1/8 in. (10 mm) wide
- Paint markers (Posca)
- Scissors
- Hot glue gun
- Big-eye beading needle

Jungle Dream Catcher

Why not recycle pretty toy animals that your children don't play with anymore and give them a new life inspired by nature? A lovely idea for decorating a child's bedroom.

LEVEL: 1 FEATHER

Prepare the materials.

2. Draw small patterns on some of the 11/16 in. (18 mm) unpolished beads with the paint markers.

3. Fix the piece of driftwood to the embroidery hoop with cotton thread, wrapping it several times around the driftwood before tying it firmly.

4. Put a drop of hot glue onto each of the animal's feet.

5. Glue the animals onto the driftwood in a row.

6. Cut 13 lengths of Jade thread: 1 of 47 1/4 in. (120 cm), 2 of 43 5/16 in. (110 cm), 2 of 39 3/8 in. (100 cm), 2 of 35 7/16 in. (90 cm), 2 of 31 1/2 in. (80 cm), 2 of 27 9/16 in. (70 cm), and 2 of 23 5/8 in. (60 cm). Fold the longest thread in two and place it in the middle. Make a loop behind the circle, thread the thread through the loop, and pull the ends. Repeat with the other lengths (from the longest to the shortest).

7. Place the glitter and satin ribbons between the strands of Jade thread and fix them onto the hoop with a drop of glue or by knotting them on.

8. Using the bead needle, slip a wooden bead onto the central strand and then add a peacock feather.

9. Alternate decorated beads, miracle beads, natural feathers, or smooth colored feathers all along the threads, minding the symmetry between the two sides.

10. Cut another length of thread and thread the tagua nut and two discs onto it. Knot it behind the central strand of the dream catcher.

11. Tie a knot at the bottom of the tagua pendant to block it. Trim all the ends of the threads.

12. Finish your creation by knotting a small piece of ribbon, adding a pretty, decorated, unpolished bead so that you can hang your dream catcher on the wall.

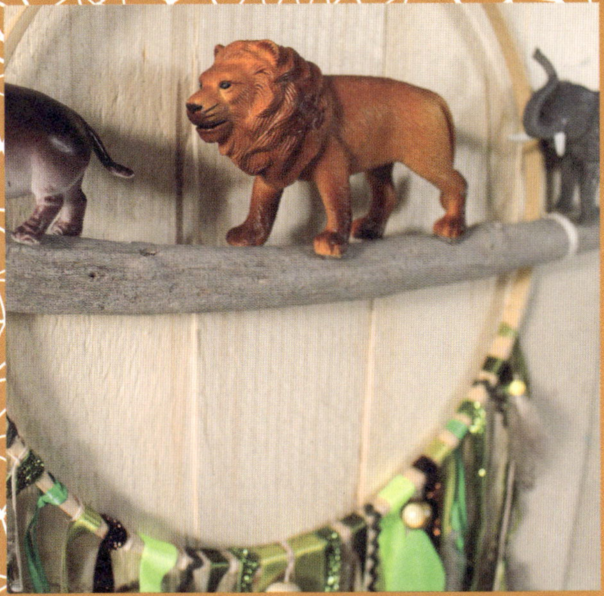
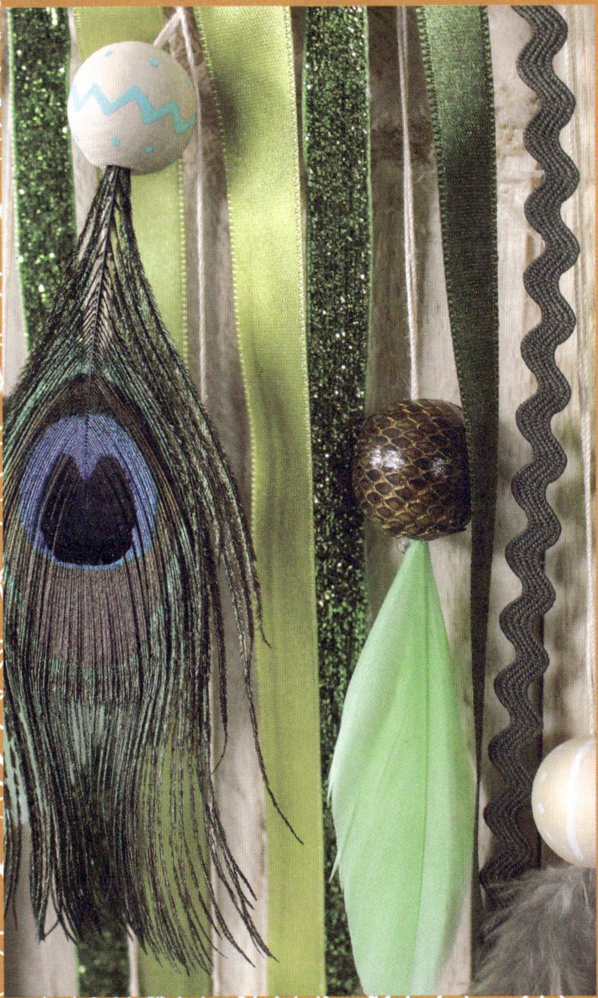
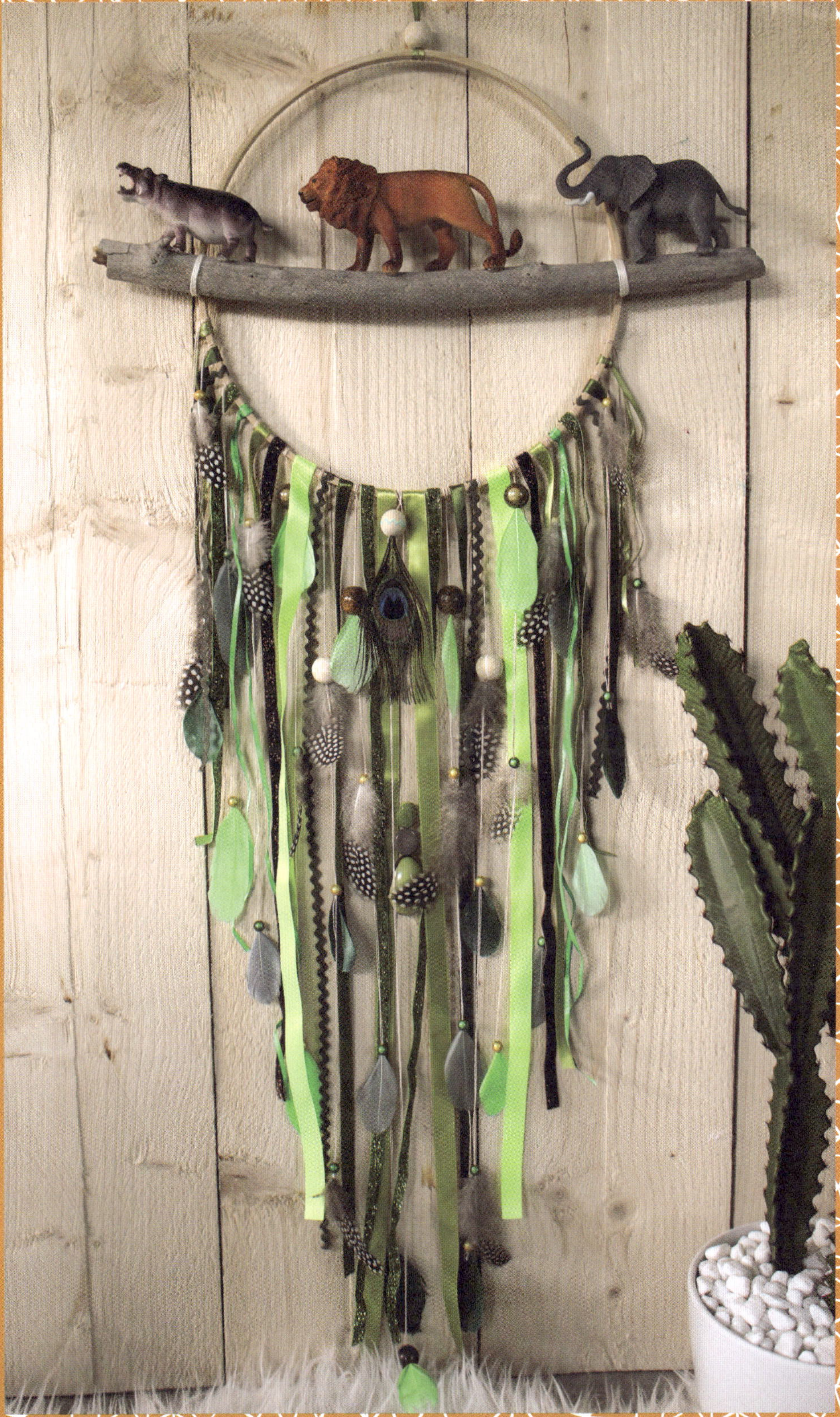

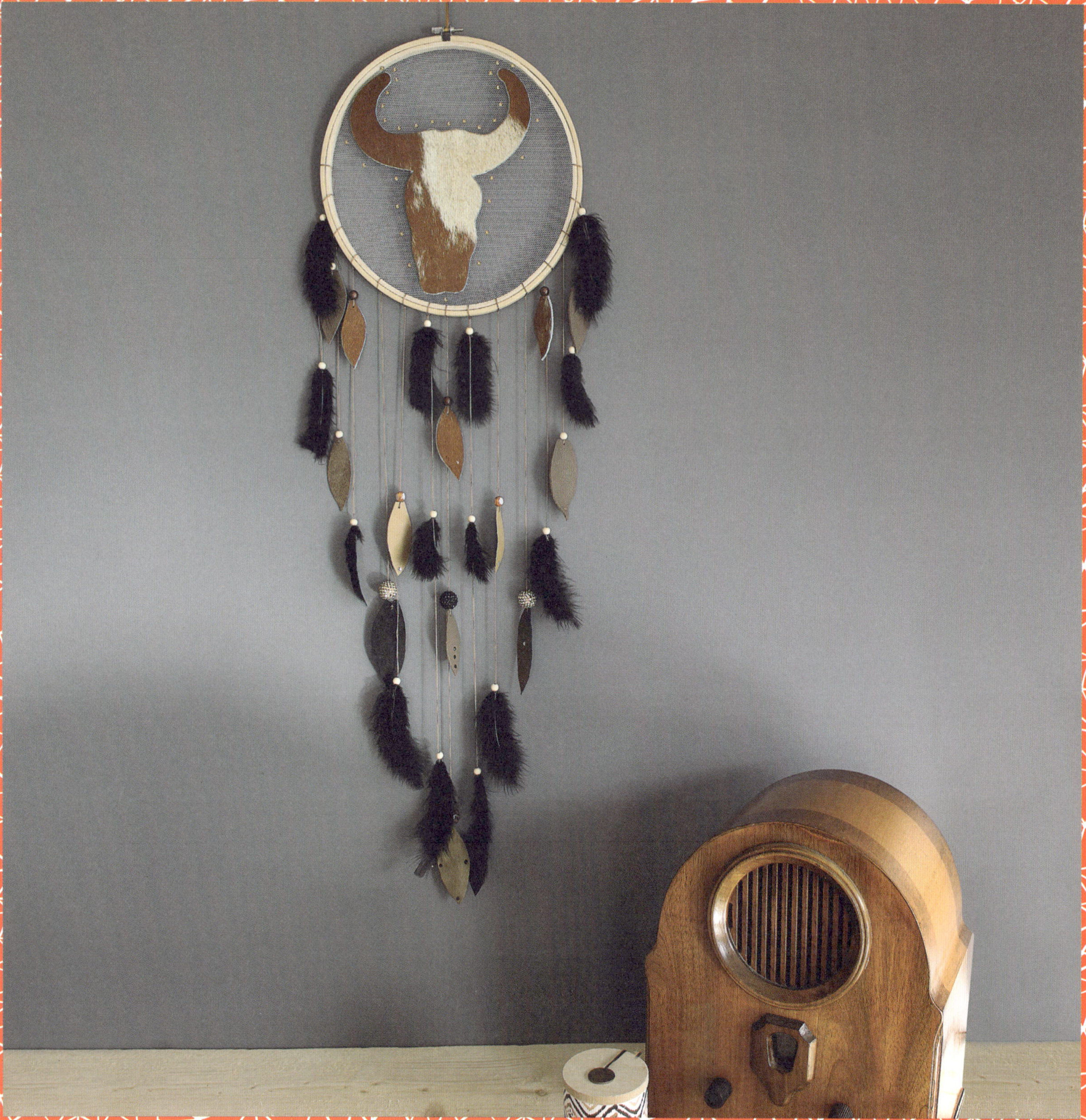

Buffalo Dream Catcher

A dream catcher with a strong character cut from lovely remnants of leather and delicately embellished with rhinestones. Ideal for warming the wooden walls of a mountain cabin!

LEVEL: 2 FEATHERS

Materials

- 1 embroidery hoop $9^{7}/_{16}$ in. (24 cm) diameter
- Tulle
- Remnants of leather or hide
- Black feathers
- Jade thread
- Wooden beads $5/_{16}$ in. (8 mm)
- Resin beads $13/_{16}$ in. (20 mm)
- Hotfix Swarovski rhinestones $3/_{16}$ in. (4 mm)
- Hotfix applicator
- Fawn-colored satin ribbon
- Dressmaker's scissors
- Punch pliers
- Hot glue gun
- Big eye beading needle
- 1 sheet of drawing paper
- Lead pencil
- Ballpoint pen
- Screwdriver

Prepare the materials.

13

2. Draw a buffalo's head on the drawing paper. Either copy a picture of one or trace it onto the paper and then cut it out.

3. Place the head onto a remnant of leather or a piece of cowhide. Trace it onto the hide with a ballpoint pen and cut it out.

4. Open your hoop and place the tulle on the half that doesn't have the screw.

5. Secure the tulle in place with the second part of the hoop, and tighten the screw with a screwdriver. Cut away the surplus tulle.

6. Put hot glue on the back of the buffalo's head using the glue gun.

7. Position the head in the center of the hoop and glue it to the tulle.

8.
Cut different-sized and colored feathers out of your remnants of leather.

9.
Prepare your Hotfix applicator with the tip size adapted to the size of the rhinestones.

10.
Once the glue is hot, glue the rhinestones onto the leather feathers you cut out earlier.

11.
Make a hole in one end of the feathers with the punch pliers.

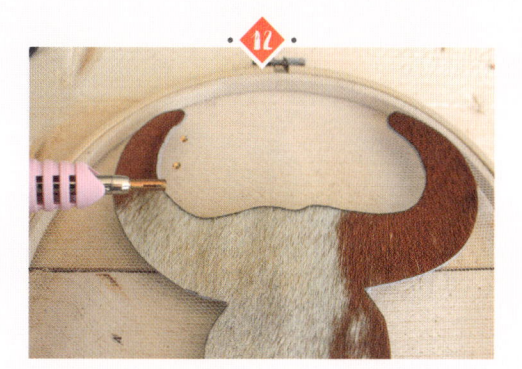

12.
Glue other rhinestones onto the tulle around the buffalo's head to add volume.

13.
Cut 1 strand of 39 3/8 in. (100 cm) Jade thread, 2 strands of 35 7/16 in. (90 cm), 2 of 31 1/2 in. (80 cm), 2 of 27 9/16 in. (70 cm), 2 of 23 5/8 in. (60 cm), 2 of 19 11/16 in. (50 cm), 2 of 15 3/4 in. (40 cm), and 2 of 11 13/16 in. (30 cm). Fold the longest strand in two and thread it through the tulle.

15

Do the same with the other strands, spreading them out according to length (from the longest to the shortest) on each side of the central strand.

Thread the wooden and resin beads all along the strands and add your leather and black downy feathers. Finish with a drop of glue to keep them in place.

Cut a short length of fawn-colored ribbon and tie it to the top of your embroidery hoop.

CHARLINE'S ADVICE

THIS MODEL CAN BE DONE IN LOTS OF OTHER PATTERNS OR SILHOUETTES! USE THE TEXTILES AND ACCESSORIES IN HARMONY WITH THE CHOSEN PATTERN.

All-Wool Dream Catcher

A soft and poetic dream catcher that combines wool, driftwood, and textile flowers. This dream catcher would be super in a little girl's bedroom or in a cozy room.

LEVEL: 2 FEATHERS

Materials

- 1 lampshade hoop 9 3/16 in. (25 cm) diameter
- Balls of wool in different colors
- 1 branch of driftwood
- Cotton thread
- Pom-pom maker (or a circle of cardboard with a hole in the middle if you don't have this practical gadget!)
- A few beads in different colors and sizes
- Textile flowers in the same colors as the wool
- Scissors
- Hot glue gun
- Bead needle
- Slide rule

Prepare the materials.

2. Tie the driftwood to the lampshade hoop with the cotton thread and cut away the extra ends.

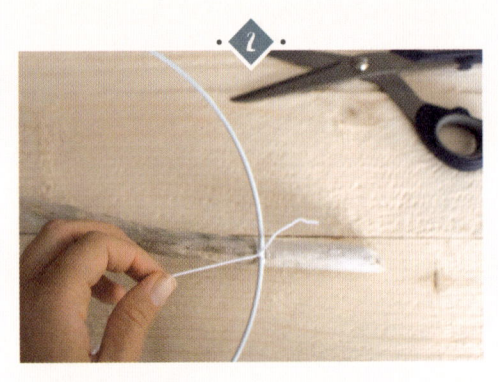

3. Cut around 50 strands 59 1/16 in. (150 cm) long from the ball of white wool. Fold them in two and attach them to the hoop, pulling them tight.

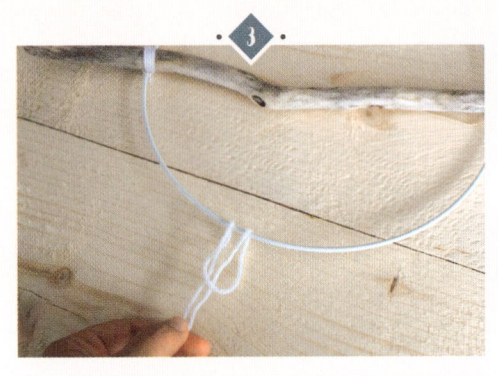

4. Cut 6 strands 59 1/16 in. (150 cm) long from another ball of wool. Attach them to the hoop in the middle of the white strands.

5. Take up 9 strands of wool and make a braid on half the total length of the strands. Make a knot with one of the strands.

6. Add beads here and there along the strands with the help of the bead needle. Don't forget to make a knot under each bead to keep it in place.

7. Put three beads of your choice (here, 2 unpolished wood beads and a rhinestone bead) onto the strands of wool left over from the braid.

8. Finish your weaving with two strands of wool (here pink) on each side of your dream catcher.

9. Place the slide rule at the bottom of the strands of wool to cut them (here slantwise) evenly.

10. Make the pom-poms: take the 2 halves of the pom-pom maker and place one against the other.

11. Wind the wool around the first hoop of the maker, pulling it tight.

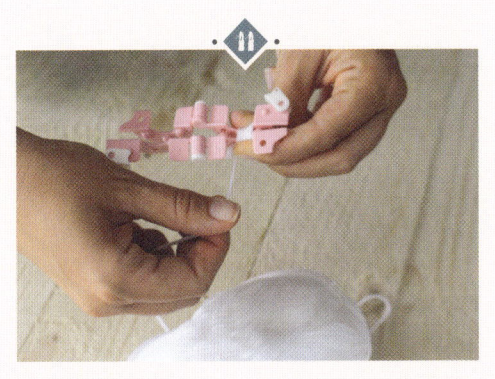

12. Cut the wool and repeat on the second loop. You'll end up with two wool "cockles."

13. Clip the two halves of the pom-pom maker together to form a single ball of wool.

19

14. Place the scissor's blade into the notch between the two parts of the pom-pom maker and cut the wool.

15. Thread a length of wool between the two sides of your pom-pom and knot it tightly.

16. Remove the pom-pom from the maker and trim with the scissors to give it a nice, round shape. Repeat until you have the desired number of pom-poms.

17. Attach your pom-poms and textile flowers to the lampshade hoop by threading silk thread through their centers.

18. To make sure they are solidly attached, add a drop of hot glue. Do the same for the textile flowers.

19. Tie a small ribbon to the top of the hoop so that you can hang your dream catcher on the wall. Add a pretty decorative pearl to embellish the ribbon.

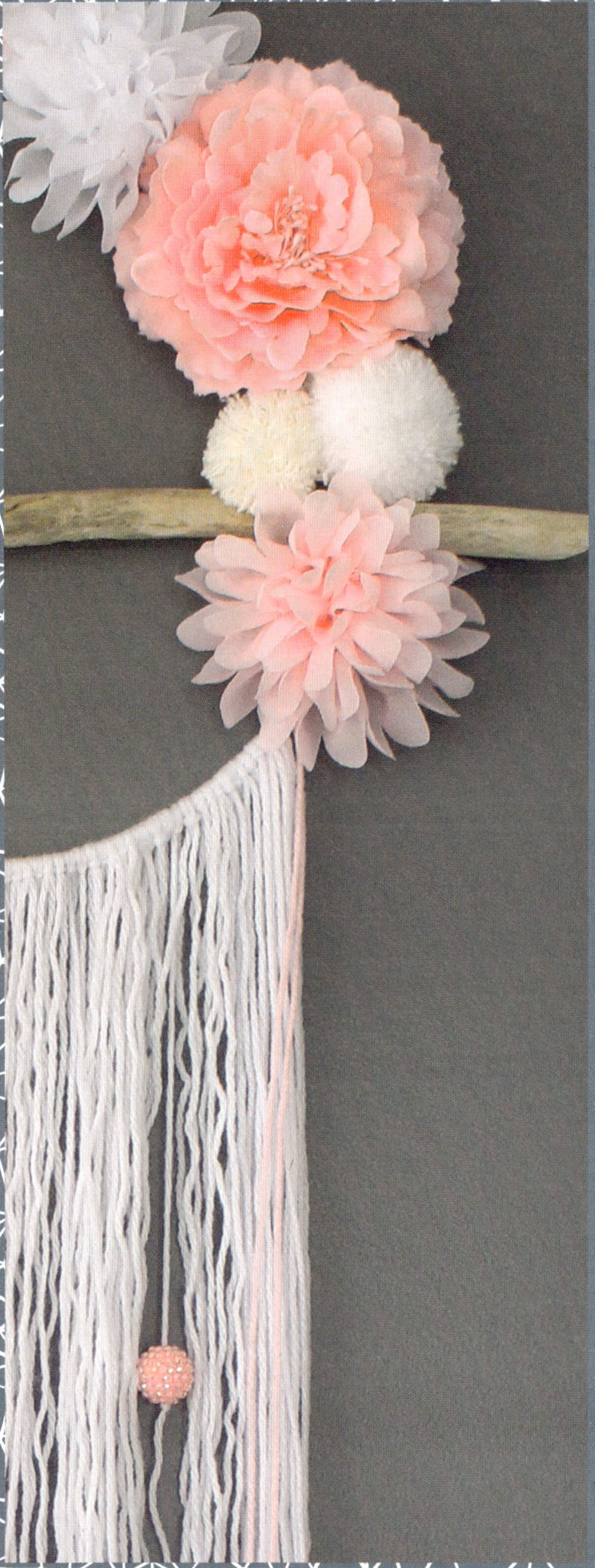

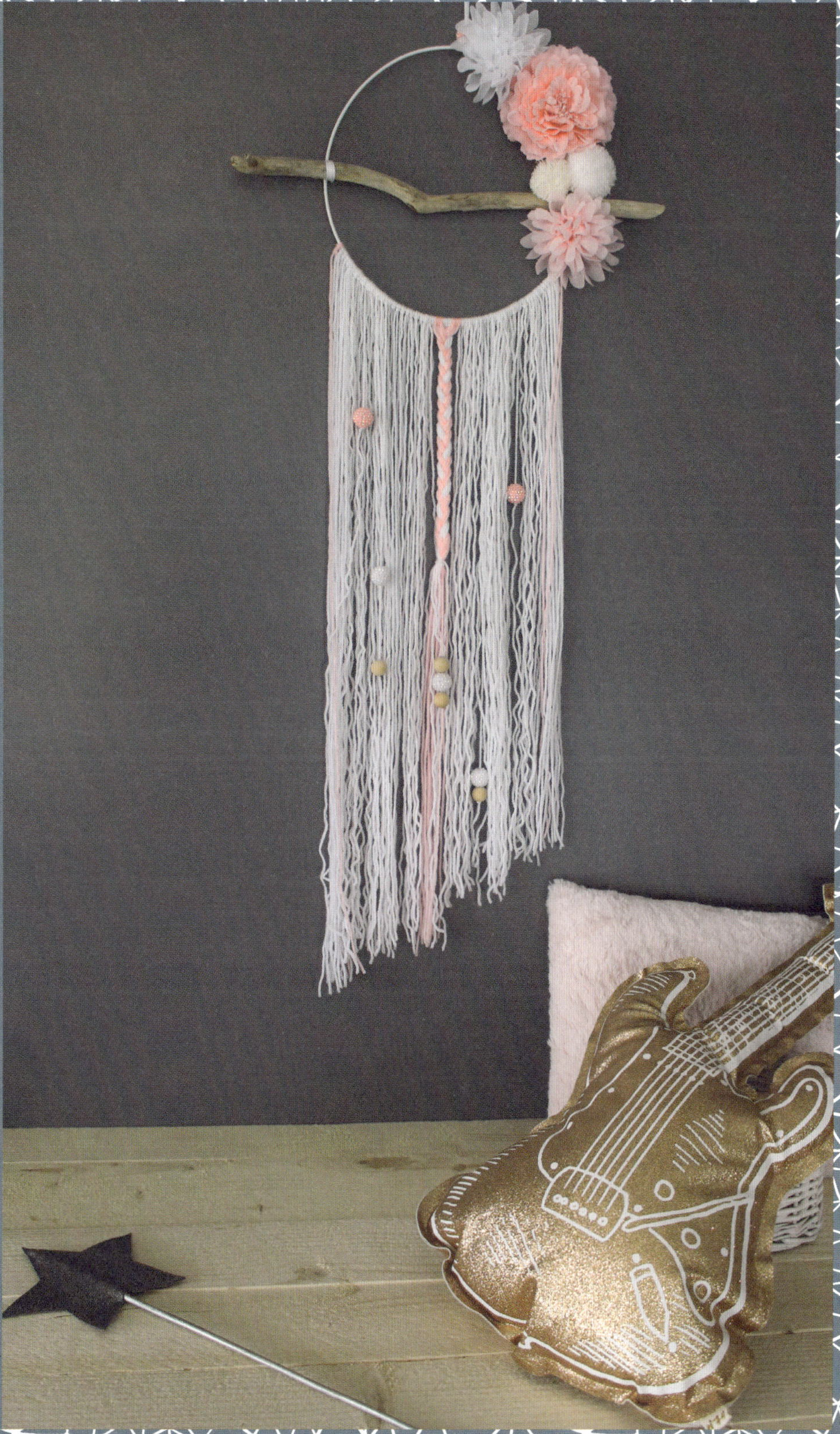

Materials

- 1 embroidery hoop 7 7/8 in. (20 cm) diameter
- 1 lace doily
- Cotton thread
- Pink and turquoise miracle beads 5/15 in. (8 mm)
- Pink and turquoise miracle beads 11/16 in. (18 mm)
- Round white resin beads 1/2 in. (12 mm) diameter
- 1 mother-of-pearl rhinestone
- Glitter ribbons in blue, pink, and yellow tones
- Satin ribbons in blue, pink, and yellow tones 1/8 in. (3 mm), 1/4 in. (6 mm), and 3/8 in. (10 mm) wide
- Pink and yellow rickrack ribbon
- Downy pink and white feathers
- Chameleon alcohol ink marker pens
- Sheets of drawing paper
- Scissors
- Hot glue gun
- Big eye beading needle
- Paper punch
- Laminator (optional)
- Laminating pouches (optional)

PAPER FEATHER DREAM CATCHER

A graphic design model inspired by the American artist Rachael Rice, who believes that working with paper is a complete form of art...The result? A fun, imaginative, and very personal dream catcher, perfect for a little girl's bedroom or a Bohemian interior.

LEVEL: 2 FEATHERS

Prepare the materials.

Use a marker to draw several feathers in different sizes, from 3 15/16 to 7 7/8 in. (10 to 20 cm) long.

Charge your markers in the mixing chamber. Color your feathers with a gradient effect.

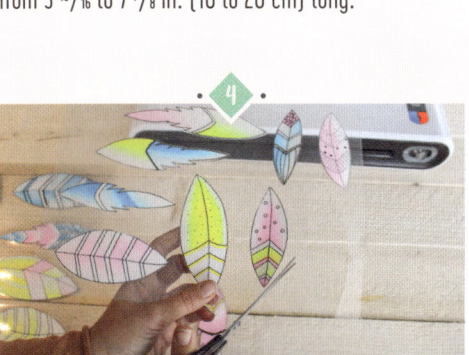

If you have a laminator, laminate your feathers. Cut around them, leaving a border of 1/8 in. (3 mm). Punch a hole in one end.

If you don't have a laminator, cut out your feathers carefully and punch a hole in one end.

Open the embroidery hoop and place the doily onto the half without the screw. Secure the lace in place with the second part of the hoop and tighten the screw. Cut away the surplus lace with dressmaker's scissors.

Cut 1 strand of 3 4/10 ft. (1 m) of cotton thread, 2 strands of 35 7/16 in. (90 cm), 2 of 31 1/2 in. (80 cm), 2 of 27 9/16 in. (70 cm), 2 of 23 5/8 in. (60 cm), 2 of 19 11/16 in. (50 cm), and 2 of 15 3/4 in. (40 cm). Tie the longest strand to the hoop and the others on each side of it, from the longest to the shortest.

Slip the miracle beads and paper feathers all along the strands, arranging them as you like. Knot the thread at each feather to keep it in place.

Cut the ends of the threads so that none stick out.

Put a drop of hot glue onto the back of the mother-of-pearl rhinestone and glue it to the center of the doily.

Then add the satin and glitter ribbons between the strands of cotton thread, fixing them to the hoop either with glue or with a knot. You can even braid some of the satin ribbons to add a little dimension to your dream catcher!

Add the downy feathers here and there by slipping the ends into the hole in the beads on the cotton threads. This will add volume and give your creation a softer touch! Finish your dream catcher by attaching a small piece of ribbon so you can hang it on the wall.

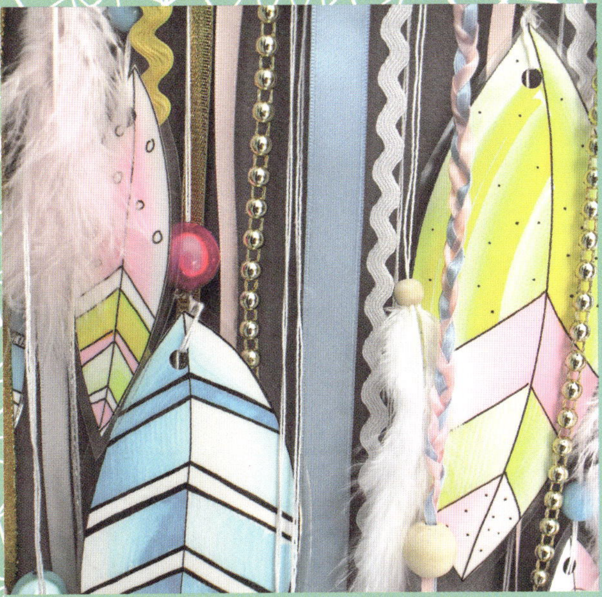
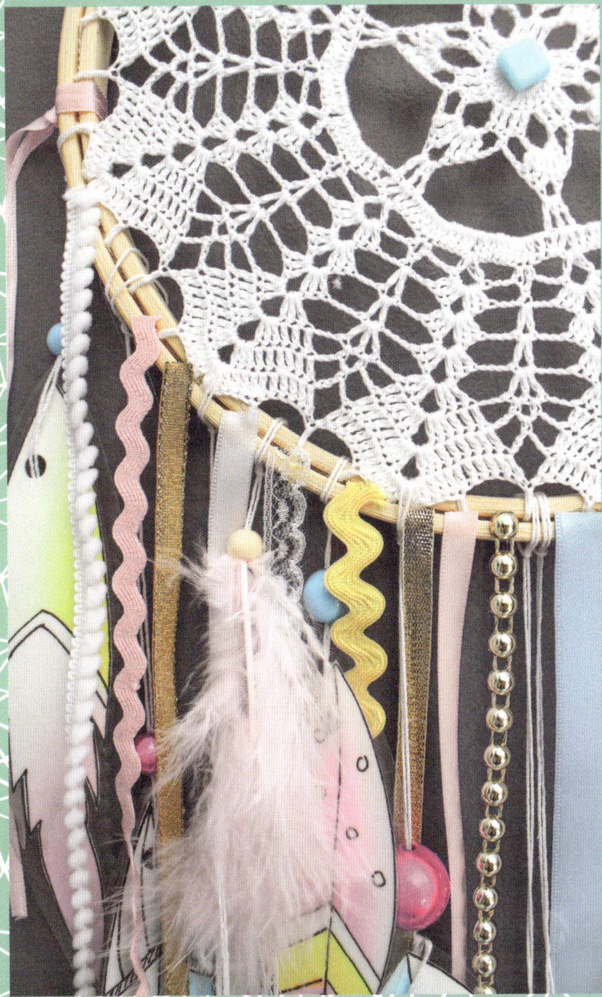
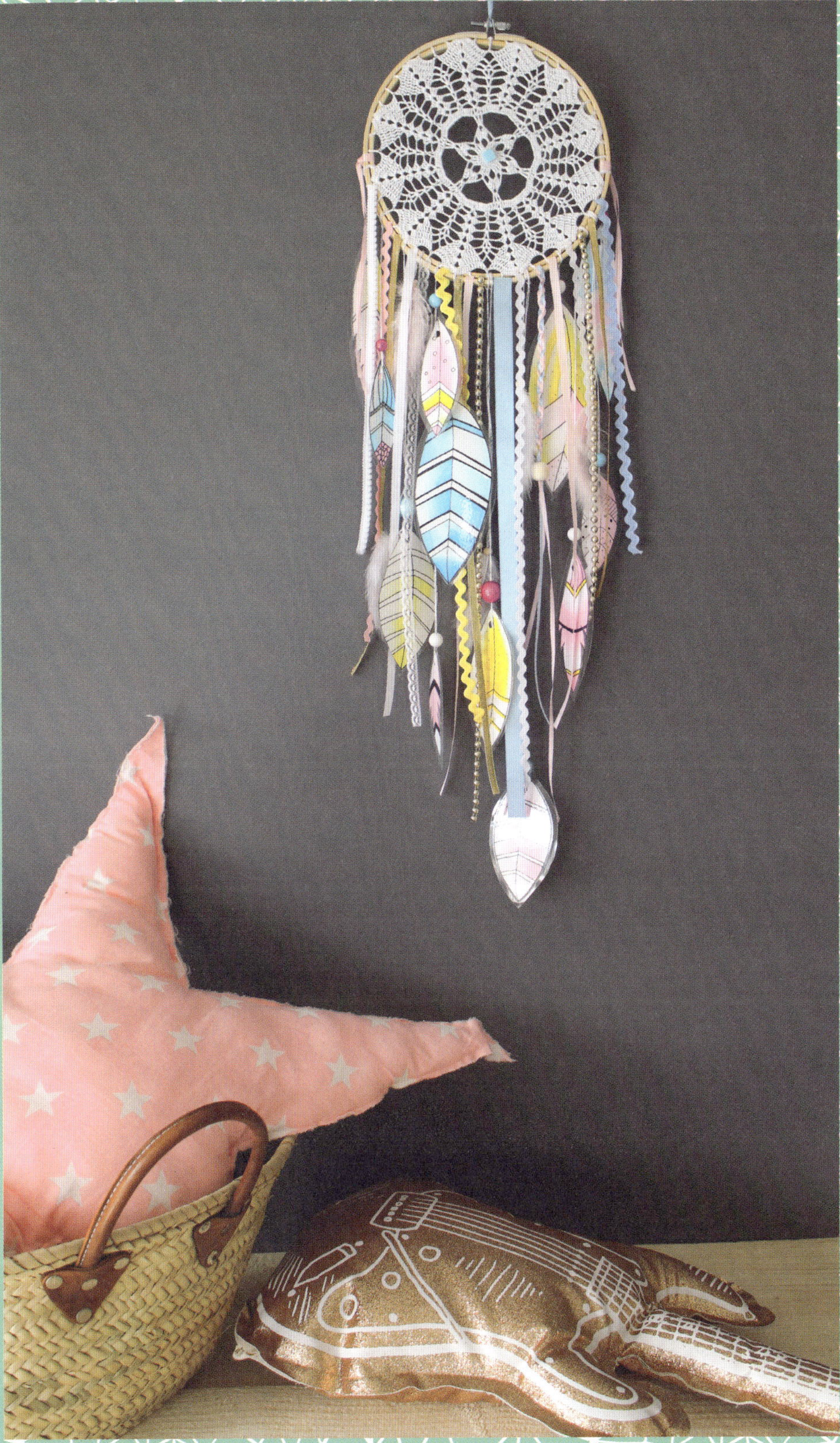

Materials

- 1 lampshade hoop 13 ¾ in. (35 cm) diameter
- 1 lovely bouquet of seasonal flowers in a harmony of colors
- 2 Gerberas
- Several blades of bear grass
- 5 glass test tubes
- 4 glass phials
- Cotton thread
- Hemp cord
- 1 small piece of satin ribbon
- Secateurs
- Hot glue gun

FLOWERY DREAM CATCHER

An extremely graceful and airy composition... A dream catcher made of fresh flowers that will make a lovely ephemeral decoration ideal for a wedding or a garden party. The secret for prolonging the joy of this decoration? The use of pretty glass phials and tubes full of water for your flowers to drink!

LEVEL: 1 FEATHER

Prepare the materials.

2. Wrap the blades of bear grass around the lampshade hoop and keep them in place with pieces of hemp cord. Make sure that the ends of the grass are at the same level.

3. Cut the ends of the flower stems so that you only have the flower.

4. Fix the flowers to the blades of bear grass and tie them in place with the cord. Repeat by placing several other flowers or bunches together.

5. Wrap a Gerbera stem all around the bear grass crown.

6. Cut other flowers and leaves and assemble them at the top of the lampshade hoop to form a uniform crown.

7. Keep everything in place with the hemp cord.

27

8. Wrap several blades of bear grass around each other to form a loop and attach it to the center of your composition.

9. Knot a small piece of satin ribbon to the center of the composition to finish decorating it.

10. Cut a short length of cotton thread and tie it to the top of the dream catcher to hang it on the wall.

11. Put a drop of glue on the top of the phials and test tubes and wind cotton thread around the top of the neck, leaving a strand about 31 1/2 in. (80 cm) long.

12. Hang your phials and test tubes from the dream catcher, knotting the threads to the hoop.

13. Cut the last flower and Gerbera stems. Fill your phials and tubes with water and put the flowers in them!

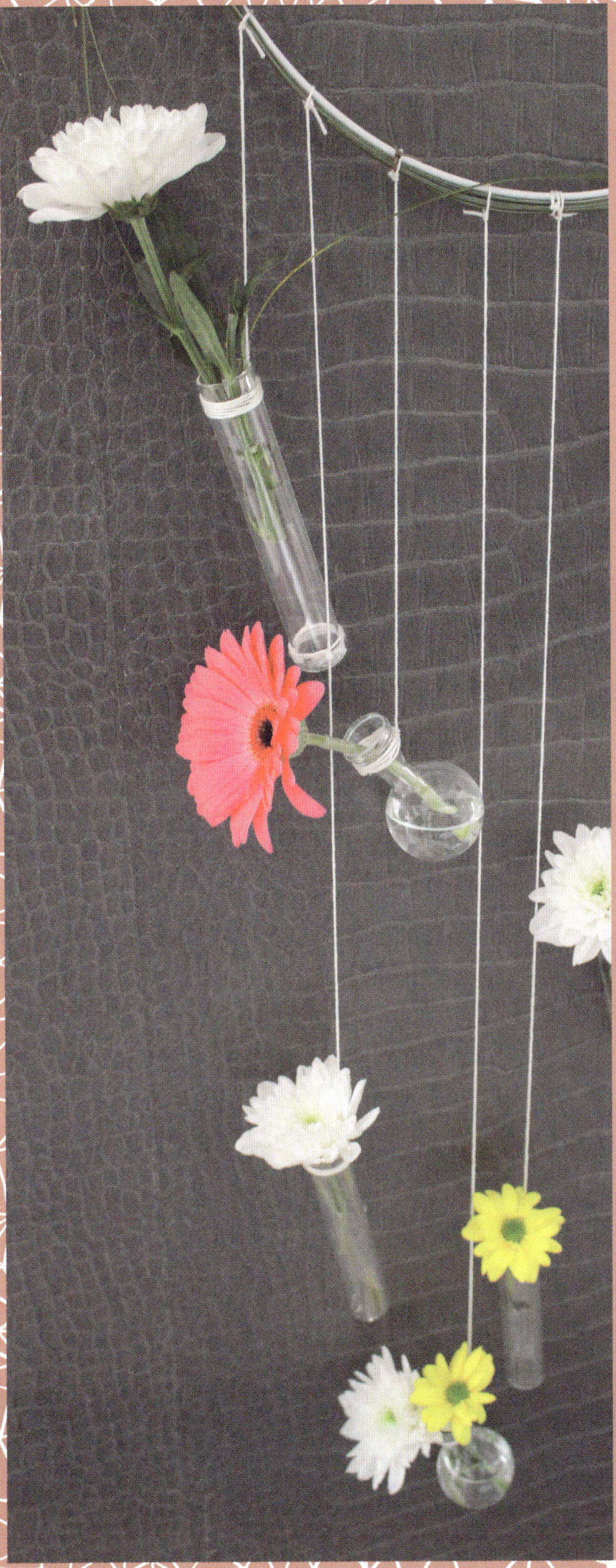
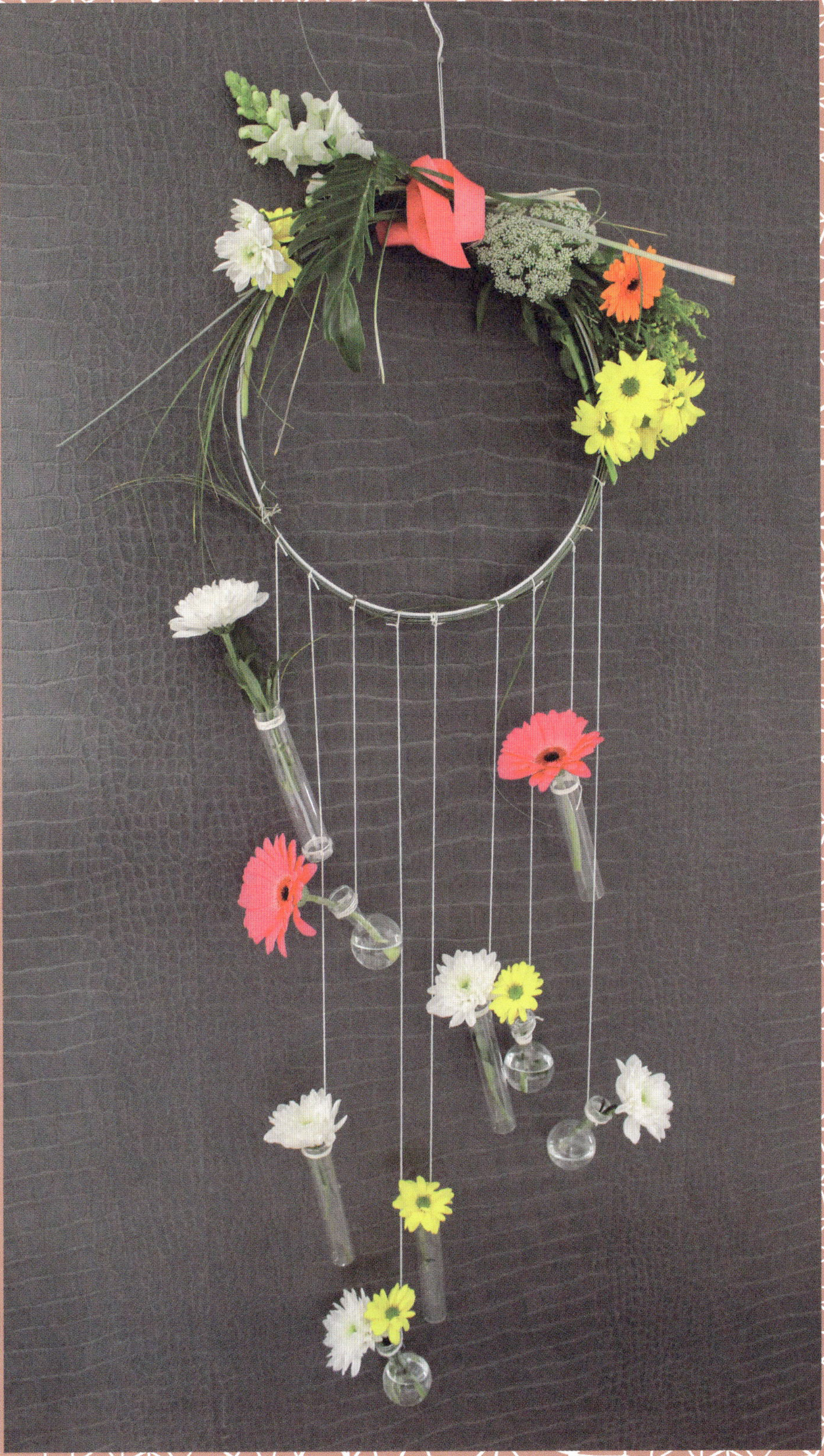

Materials

- 1 embroidery hoop 9 7/16 in. (24 cm) diameter
- Remnants of leather and imitation leather in copper, mustard, and brown shades
- Jade thread
- A few natural feathers in brown tones (guineafowl, pheasant, peacock feathers...)
- Several polished and unpolished wooden beads 11/16 in. (18 mm)
- 1 tagua nut 1 3/8 to 2 3/16 in. (35 to 55 mm) natural color
- 1 howlite leaf bead
- Several unpolished heishi beads 3/16 in. (4 mm)
- Several açai seed beads
- Glitter glue
- Loose glitter
- Ribbon
- Punch pliers
- Scissors
- Hot glue gun
- Big-eye beading needle

Amerindian Dream Catcher

A STYLE THAT EVOKES TRADITION IN A MODERN SPIRIT...

LEVEL: 3 FEATHERS

Prepare the materials.

2. Use the inner circle of the embroidery hoop.

3. Cut about 13 ft. (4 m) of Jade thread and tie one end to the hoop.

4. Pull the thread to the other side of the circle and tie it on.

5. Continue in the same way in diagonals, securing the thread each time with a knot.

6. Repeat as many times as you like, giving your imagination free rein. However, don't do all the weaving at this stage.

7. Use the bead needle to thread a bead onto the Jade thread.

8. Continue weaving, adding on a bead from time to time to enliven the center of your dream catcher.

9. Finish your weaving with a last knot and secure it with a drop of hot glue.

10. Cut 1 strand of 47 1/4 in. (120 cm) of Jade thread. Then 2 strands of 43 5/16 in. (110 cm), 2 of 39 3/8 in. (100 cm), 2 of 35 7/16 in. (90 cm), 2 of 31 1/2 in. (80 cm), 2 of 27 9/16 in. (70 cm), and 2 of 23 5/8 in. (60 cm). Tie the 47 1/4 in. (120 cm) strand to the circle with a sliding knot.

11. Place the rest of the strands on each side of the central one, from the longest to the shortest.

12. Cut out pretty textile feathers from the remnants of leather and imitation leather using the dressmaker's scissors. You can cut small fringes on each feather to give them more volume.

13. Punch a hole in one end of each feather with the punch pliers.

14
Apply a little glitter glue in the shape of a triangle on the tip of the white feathers.

15
Dunk each feather into a bowl of loose glitter and then shake the feather to remove the excess.

16
Use the bead needle to thread beads onto the strands and slip the quills of the feathers into the beads' holes, alternating the feathers as you go along.

17
Put a drop of hot glue between the quill and the bead to bind them solidly together. Add more beads and feathers to the strands of thread.

18
Cut another length of thread and slip on the tagua nut and a few açai seed beads and tie a knot.

19
Use the cutting pliers to snip off the ends of the quills that are sticking out of the top of the beads.

Tie a short piece of ribbon to the top of your dream catcher so you can hang it on the wall. Your dream catcher, with its pretty central weave, is now finished. It's ready to capture all your dreams!

CHARLINE'S ADVICE

TO CREATE A PERSONALIZED MODEL, YOU CAN USE ALPHABET BEADS IN THE CENTER OF THE WEAVE TO MAKE A WORD OR A NAME!

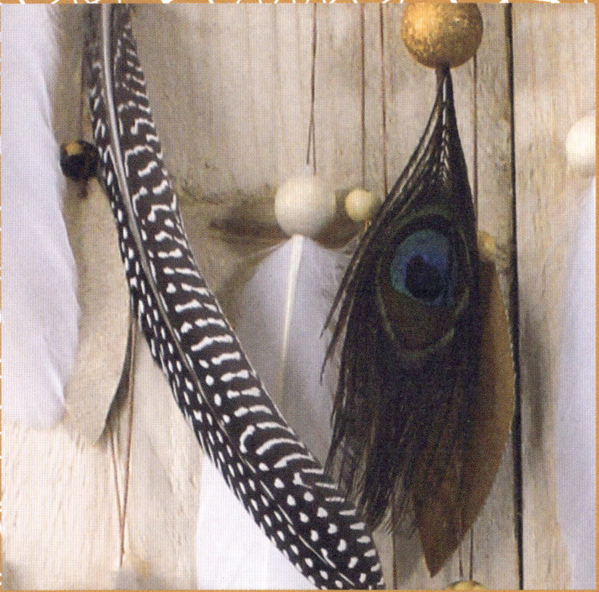
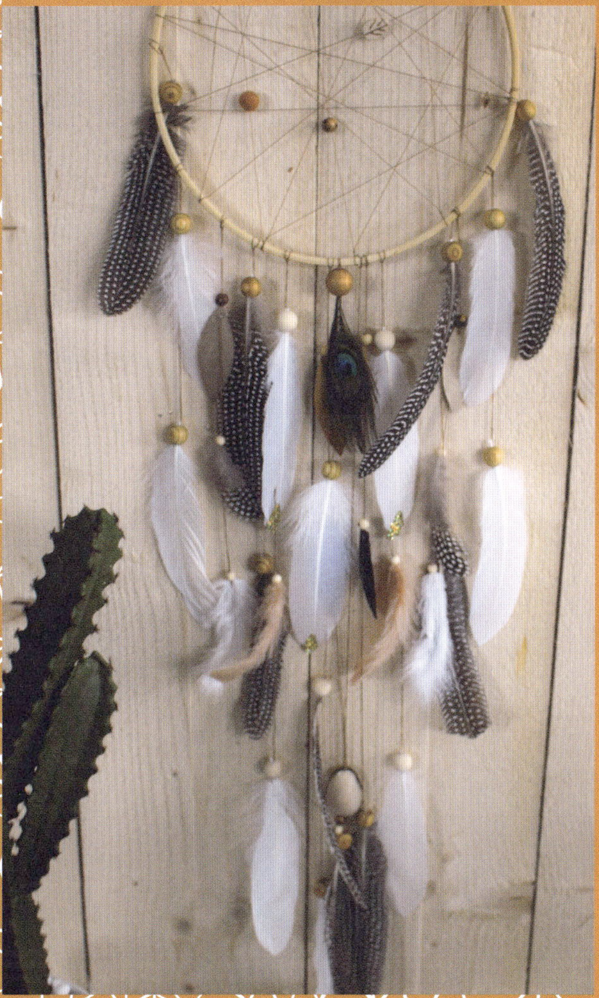
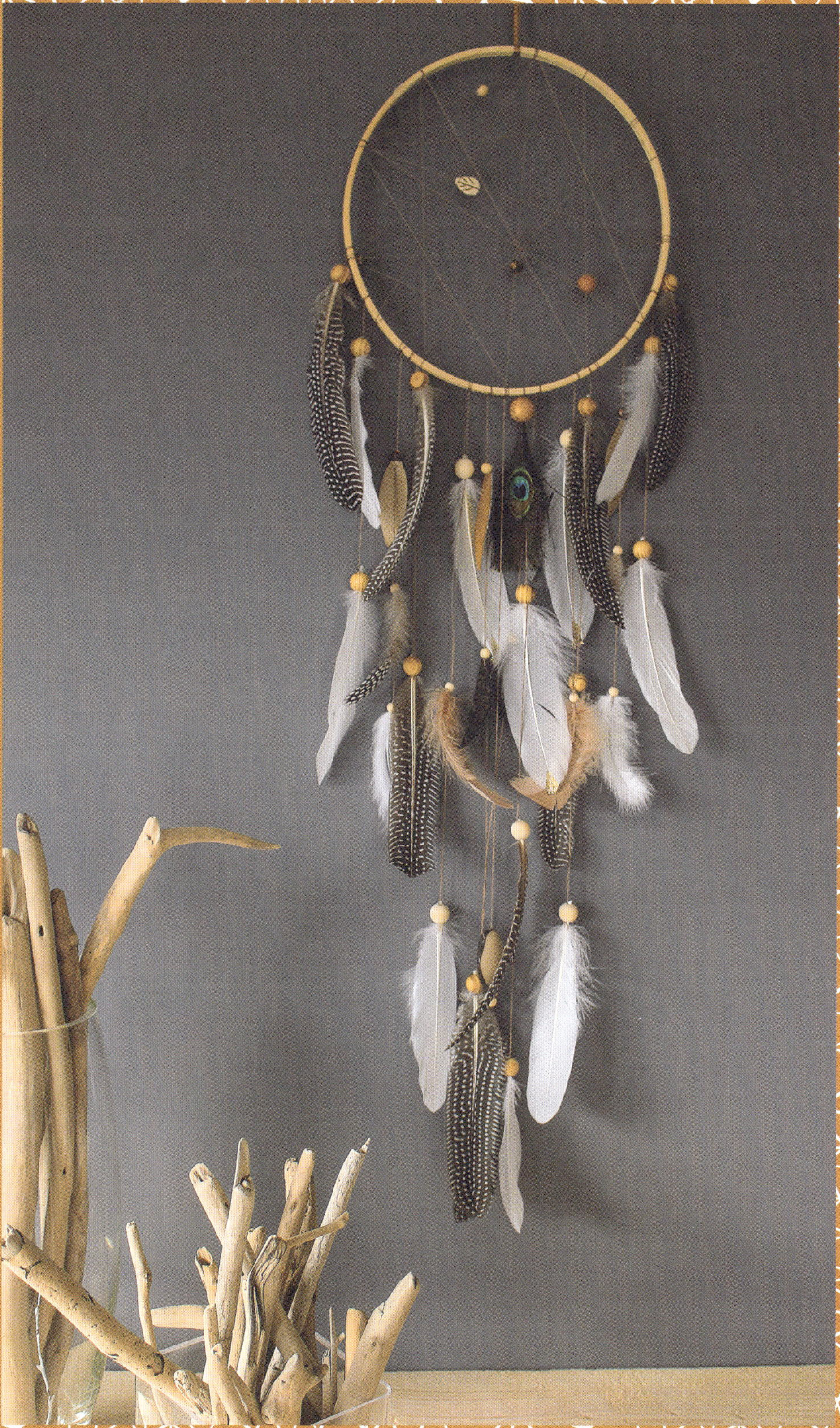

Materials

- 1 embroidery hoop 6 11/16 in. (17 cm) diameter
- 1 crocheted lace doily 8 11/16 in. (22 cm) diameter
- 1 bag of white feathers
- Cotton thread
- Several white or transparent glass beads
- 1 mother-of-pearl rhinestone
- 3 Swarovski crystal cabochons
- Several resin beads 5/16 in. (8 mm) diameter
- 1 white satin ribbon
- Scissors
- Hot glue gun
- Big-eye beading needle
- Screwdriver

Sophisticated Dream Catcher

This is a very refined dream catcher combining fine lace, airy feathers, and delicate glass and crystal beads. It is a truly sophisticated little gem of a dream catcher that will turn your room into a jewelry box!

LEVEL: 3 FEATHERS

Prepare the materials.

36

· 2 ·

Open the embroidery hoop and place the lace doily onto the part without the screw.

· 3 ·

Secure the doily with the second part of the hoop and tighten it using a screwdriver. Cut away the surplus lace.

· 4 ·

Put a drop of glue onto the back of the mother-of-pearl rhinestone and glue it to the center of the doily.

· 5 ·

Cut 1 strand of 23 5/8 in. (60 cm) of cotton thread, then 2 of 19 11/16 in. (50 cm), 2 of 15 3/4 in. (40 cm), 2 of 11 13/16 in. (30 cm), and 2 of 7 7/8 in. (20 cm). Fold the longest thread in two, make a loop behind the hoop and pull the thread tight to secure it to the hoop.

· 6 ·

Do the same with the other threads on each side of the central one, from the longest to the shortest.

· 7 ·

With your bead needle, thread a large bead onto the central strand.

8. Now slip as many glass beads as you like onto this strand, ending with one of the crystal cabochons.

9. Skip two strands on each side of the central one and repeat steps 7 and 8 on the third strands.

10. For the remaining strands: thread on a white resin bead and push it up to the top of the strand. Tie a knot under it to keep it in place.

11. Push the quill of a white feather into the bead's hole and secure it with a drop of hot glue.

12. Thread another bead onto the bottom of the strand and tie a knot under it. Cut away the surplus thread.

13. Cut off a short length of white satin ribbon and knot it to the top of the embroidery hoop.

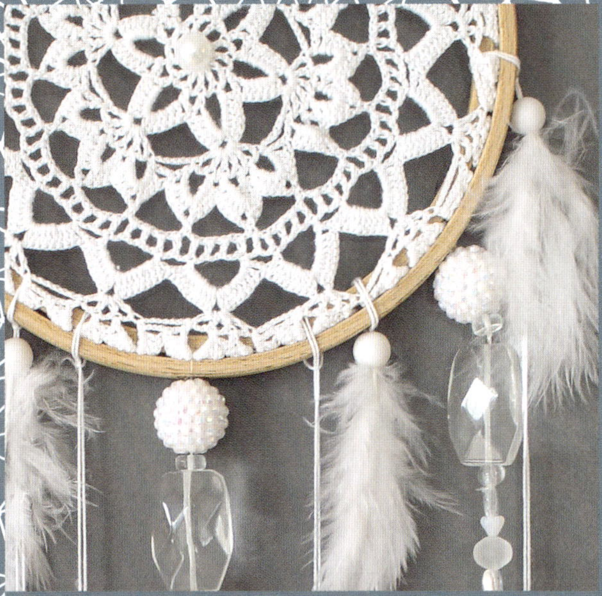
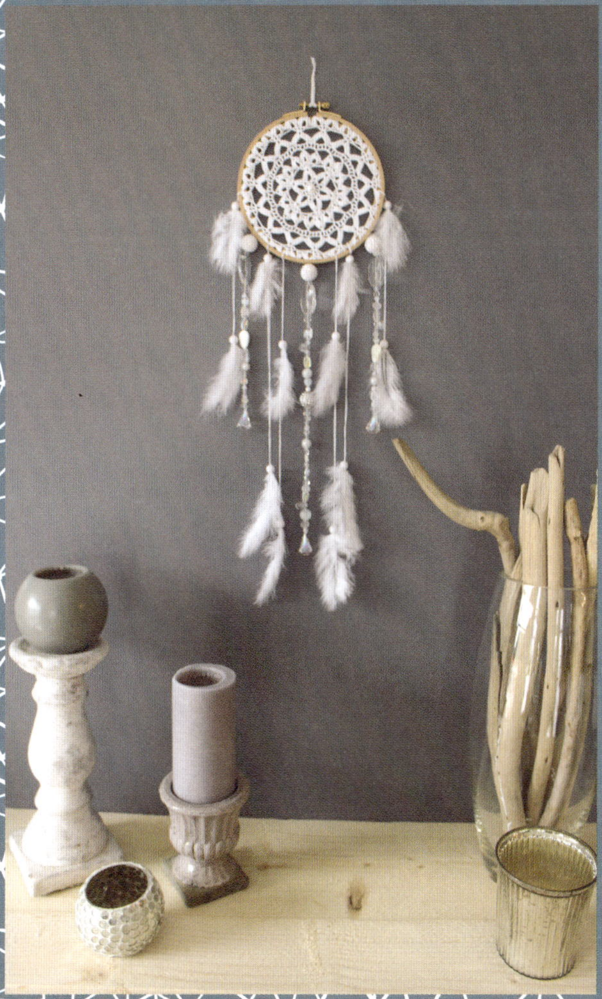
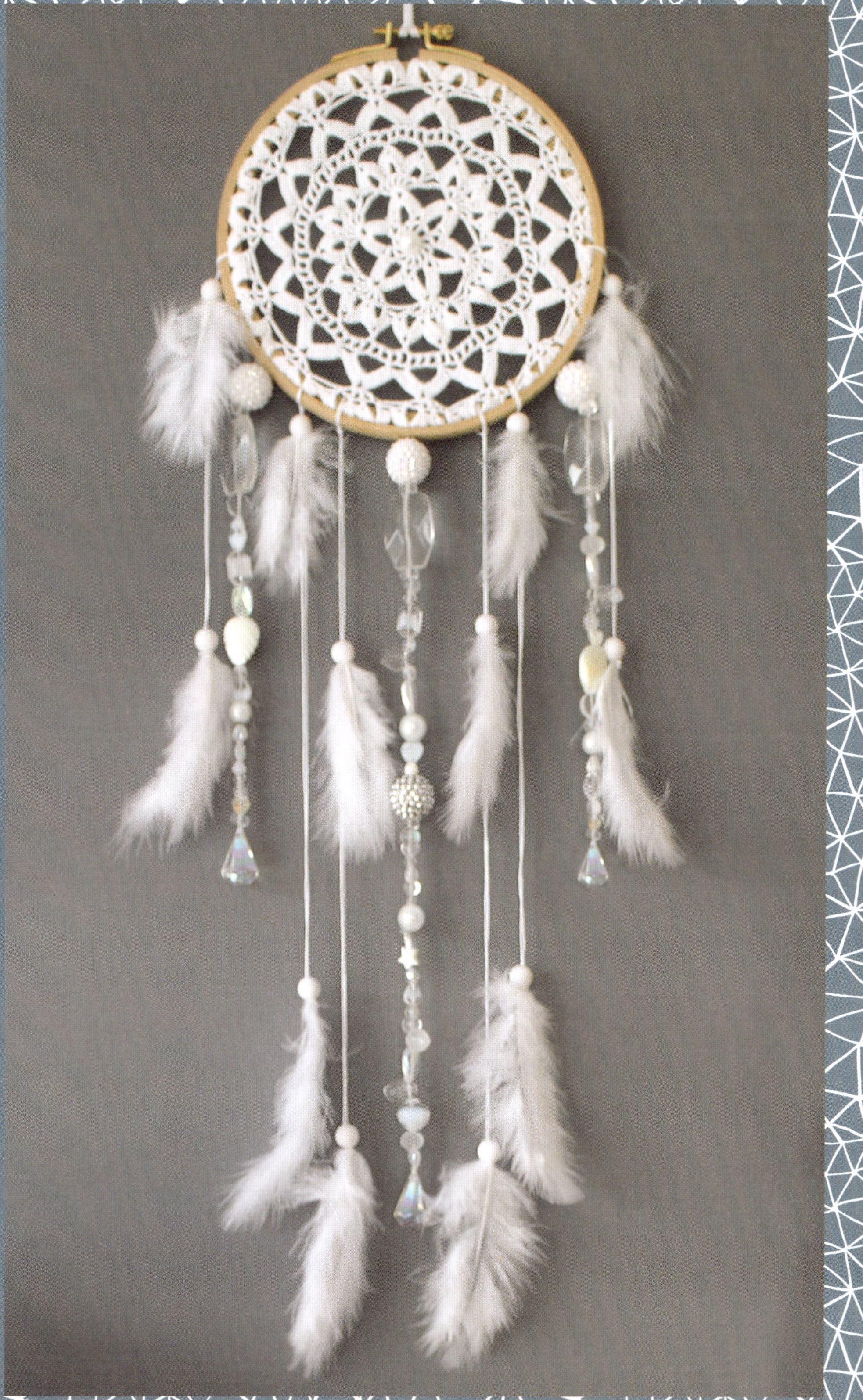

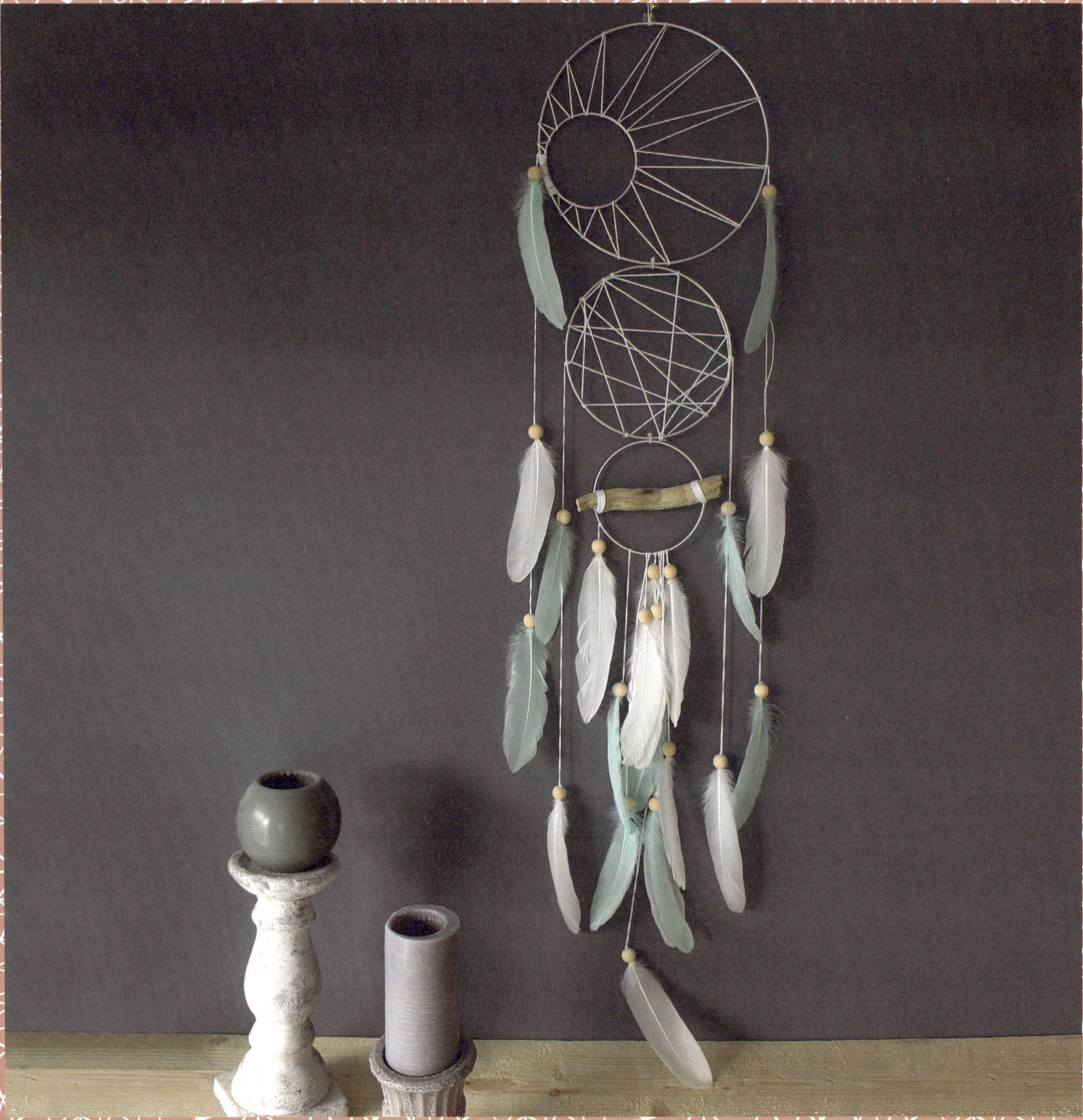

Triple-Weave Dream Catcher

Spectacular!
An unusual dream catcher that combines different weaving techniques that will certainly add a bohemian air to your decoration. . . .

Level: 3 feathers

Prepare the materials.

Materials

- 4 lampshade hoops in different diameters: 11 13/16 in. (30 cm), 7 7/8 in. (20 cm), 5 15/16 in. (15 cm), and 3 15/16 in. (10 cm)
- Cotton thread
- White yarn
- White and aqua green feathers
- Unpolished wooden beads 11/16 in. (18 mm)
- 1 piece of driftwood
- Scissors
- Cutting pliers
- Hot glue gun
- Big eye beading needle
- 2 adjustable plastic clamps 1 in. (2.5 cm)

2.

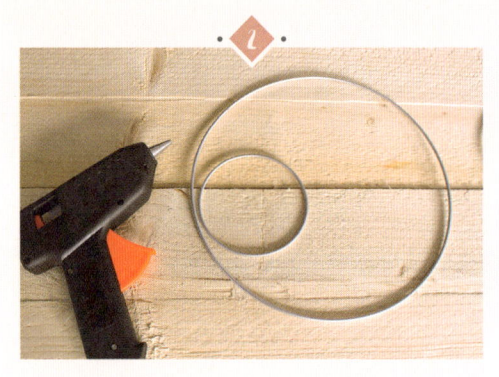

Place the 3 15/16 in. (10 cm) hoop inside the 11 13/16 in. (30 cm) hoop.

3.

Cut about 9 ft. 10 1/8 in. (3 m) of white yarn and attach the two hoops together with a few inches/centimeters of the yarn. Finish by adding a drop of hot glue.

4.

Wind the rest of the yarn around the 2 circles to make yarn rays. To keep them in place either knot them or glue them.

5.

Tie the piece of driftwood to the 5 15/16 in. (15 cm) hoop with cotton thread.

6.

Cut around 9 ft. 10 1/8 in. (3 m) of white yarn. Tie one end to the 7 7/8 in. (20 cm) hoop.

7.

Pull it across to the opposite side of the hoop and tie a knot.

42

8. Continue to pull your yarn diagonally, from one side of the hoop to the other, tying a knot each time to secure the weave.

9. Finish your weaving with a last knot and secure it with a drop of hot glue.

10. Join the first and second hoops with an adjustable plastic clamp.

11. Cut the end of the clamp with the cutting pliers.

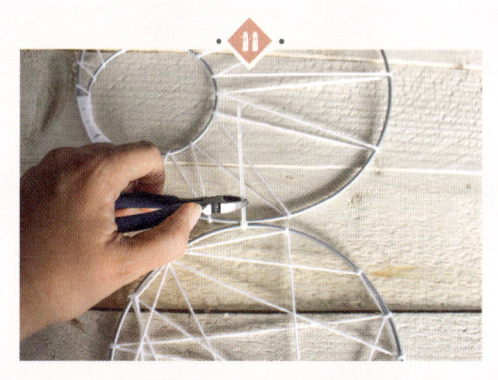

12. Repeat to attach the other hoop.

13. Cut 4 pieces of cotton thread about 59 1/16 in. (150 cm) long. Knot these to the first two woven hoops.

14. Now tie 9 threads 27 9/16 in. (70 cm) long to the smaller hoop with the driftwood in the center.

15. Thread 3 wooden beads and feathers onto the first 4 strands of your dream catcher, alternating white and aqua green feathers.

16. Repeat with wooden beads and feathers on the strands of the third hoop. Use the cutting pliers to cut the ends of the feathers that stick out of the top of the beads. Glue the feathers to the beads with hot glue.

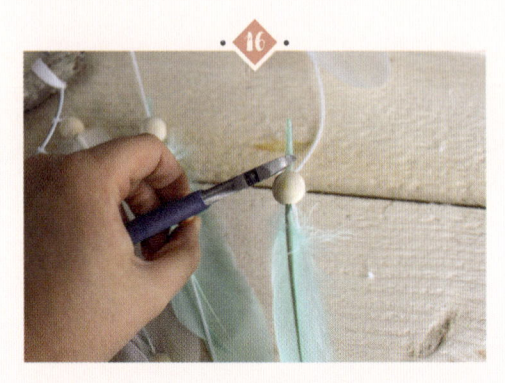

17. Tie on a small ribbon to the first hoop to hang the dream catcher on the wall.

× CHARLINE'S ADVICE ×

YOU CAN USE COLORED YARN FOR THE WEAVE. THIS WILL ADD A TOUCH OF ORIGINALITY TO YOUR PIECE!

ROMANTIQUE WALL HANGING

A lovely and original decoration for a stairwell or the wall behind your bed. Give your imagination free rein to make a wall hanging that reflects your spirit!

LEVEL: FEATHER

Materials

- 8 embroidery hoops in different diameters: 4 of 5 1/8 in. (13 cm), 2 of 9 7/16 in. (24 cm), and 2 of 7 7/8 in. (20 cm)
- 5 crocheted lace doilies in different diameters
- Remnants of imitation leather
- 1 driftwood branch
- Fishing twine
- Cotton thread
- 5 adjustable plastic clamps 1 in. (2.5 cm)
- 2 screw-in eye hooks
- Cutting pliers
- Hot glue gun
- Screwdriver
- Lead pencil

Prepare the materials.

45

Open a 5 1/8 in. (13 cm) hoop and place a doily on the part without the screw.

Secure the doily with the second part of the hoop and tighten the screw with a screwdriver.

Cut away the surplus lace. Repeat with the rest of the doilies choosing hoops of different diameters.

Secure a piece of imitation leather in one of the hoops.

Cut away the surplus leather. Repeat with two other pieces of imitation leather to obtain 3 hoops decorated with imitation leather.

Place the different hoops side by side and decide how you want to arrange them.

8. Make a pencil mark on the doily hoops to indicate the place for the clamps.

9. Join the first two hoops together with a clamp.

10. Cut the end of the clamp with the cutting pliers for a neat finish.

11. Repeat with all the doily hoops.

12. Place the imitation leather hoops between the doily hoops and fix them with hot glue: they can't be secured with clamps.

13. Press the hoops together while the glue is drying.

14. Screw the eye hooks into the branch of driftwood.

15. Cut a length of thread and tie each end to the eye hooks.

16. Cut out three bands of about 2 in. (5 cm) of imitation leather and glue them to the branch of driftwood.

17. Cut several lengths of fishing twine and use them to tie the hoops to the driftwood.

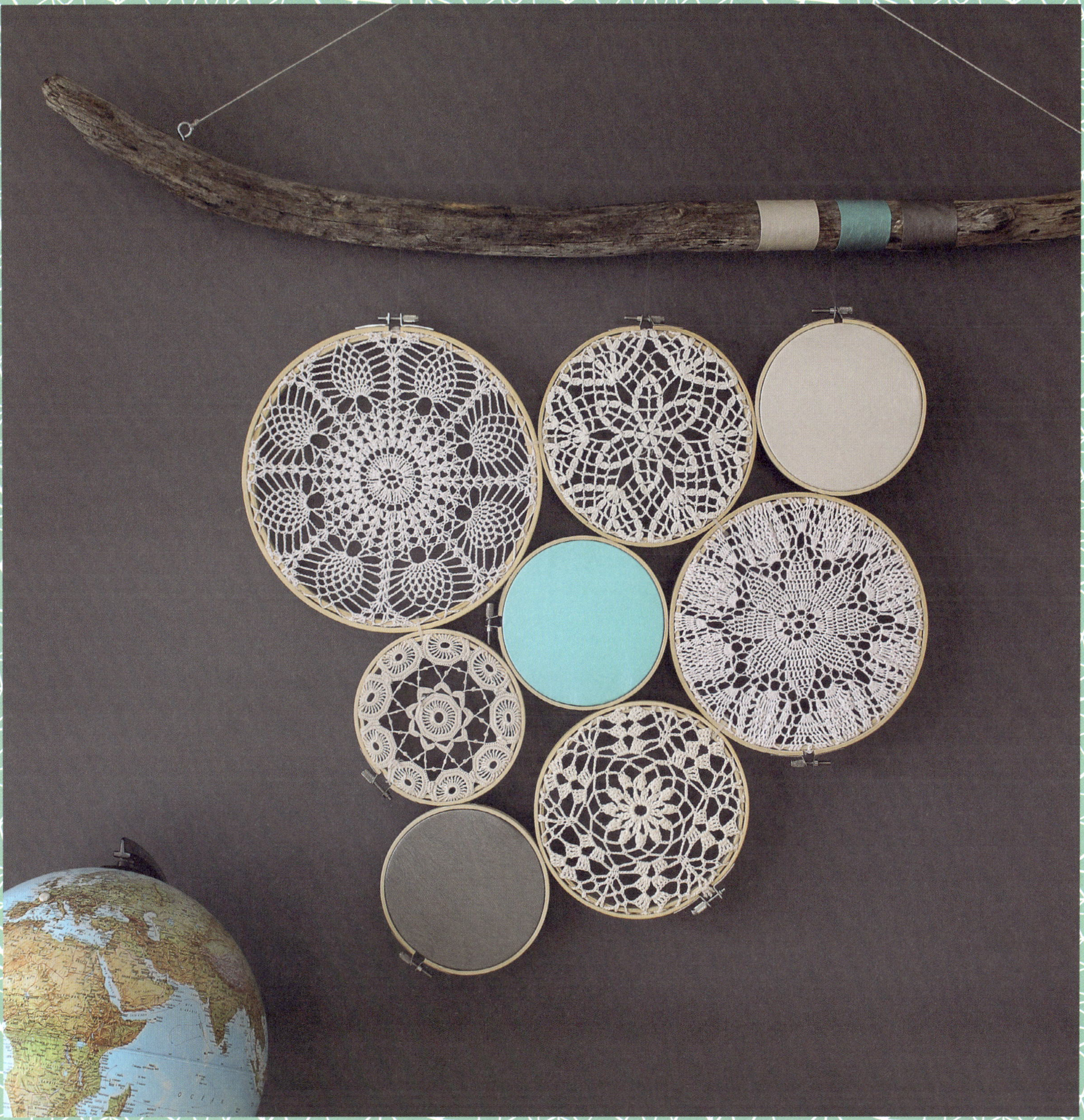

Materials

- A driftwood branch about 3 ft. 3 3/8 in. (1 m) long
- Small driftwood branches
- Shells and objects that invoke the sea
- Beads in different sizes and textures
- 3 polished turquoise tagua nuts 1 3/8 to 2 in. (35 to 50 mm)
- Transparent plastic teardrops and baubles
- Decorative sand
- Fishing twine
- Cotton thread
- 2 screw-in eye hooks
- Scissors
- Cutting pliers
- Hot glue gun
- Drill

MARINE WALL HANGING

A WALL HANGING THAT HAS A SUMMERY FEEL AND SOUVENIRS OF YOUR VACATIONS IN THE SUN! A NATURAL DECORATION THAT WILL HIGHLIGHT LITTLE TREASURES FOUND ON THE BEACH...

LEVEL: 2 FEATHERS

Prepare the materials.

50

· 2 ·

Screw the two eye hooks into the branch of driftwood.

· 3 ·

Cut a length of cotton thread and tie the ends to the hooks.

· 4 ·

Pour a little sand into the teardrops.

· 5 ·

Fill the teardrops and baubles with all the treasures you have picked up on the beach (shells, small branches of driftwood) or with pretty objects that remind you of the sea.

· 6 ·

Drill a hole in the middle of the small driftwood branches.

· 7 ·

Do the same with the largest shells. Be careful! They are very fragile, so drill slowly, holding them firmly in place.

51

8. Cut 2 lengths of fishing twine 3 ft. 3 3/8 in. (1 m) long. Thread the small branches onto one of the lengths of twine and tie a knot.

9. Continue, alternating branches, shells, beads, and tagua nuts all along the twine.

10. Carry on until you have a garland of driftwood around 27 9/16 in. (70 cm) long.

11. Do the same with the second length of twine, making another garland.

12. Thread fishing twine through the top of the teardrops and baubles filled with your pretty treasures. Add a few beads to decorate the tops.

13. Tie your garlands to each end of the driftwood branch and hang your teardrops and baubles.

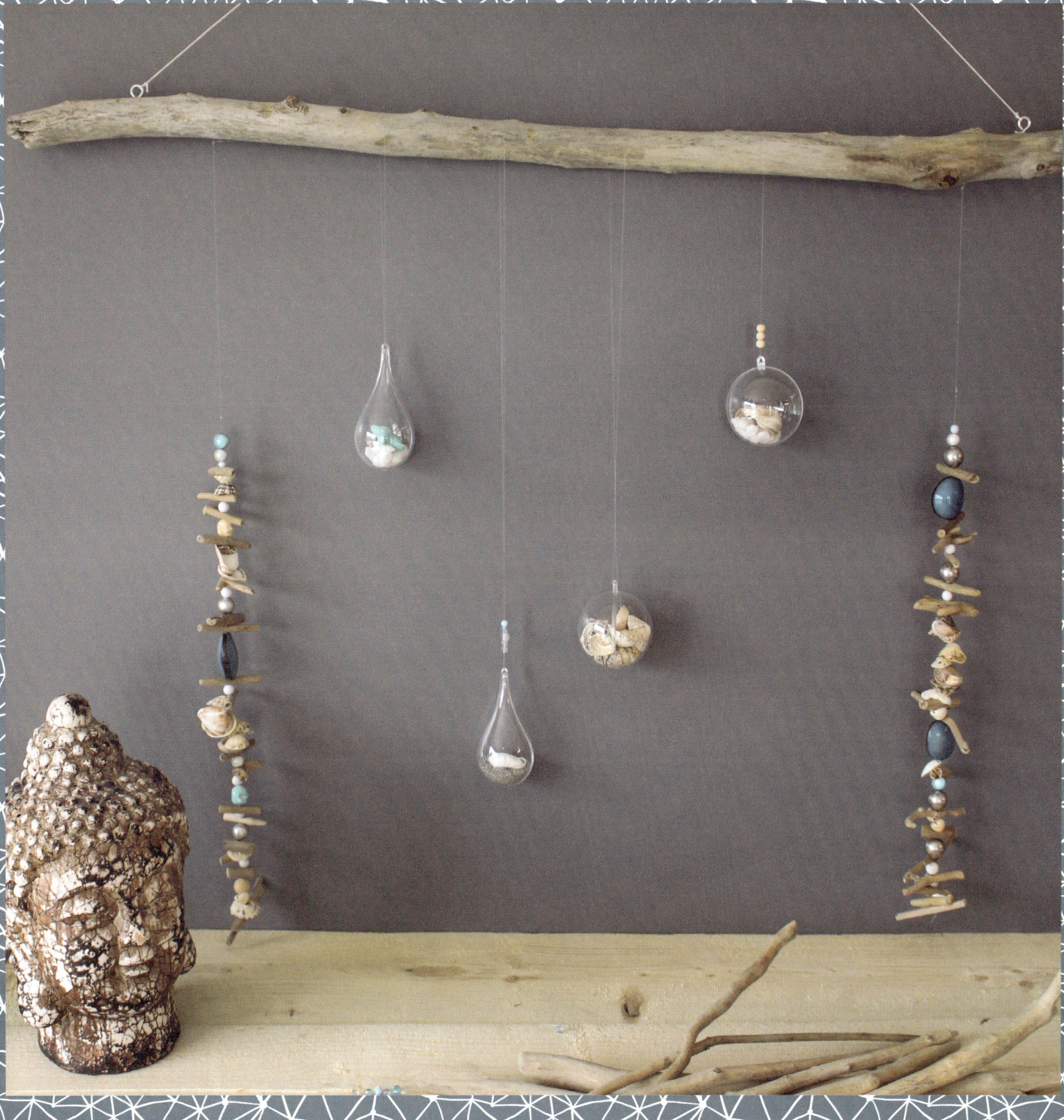

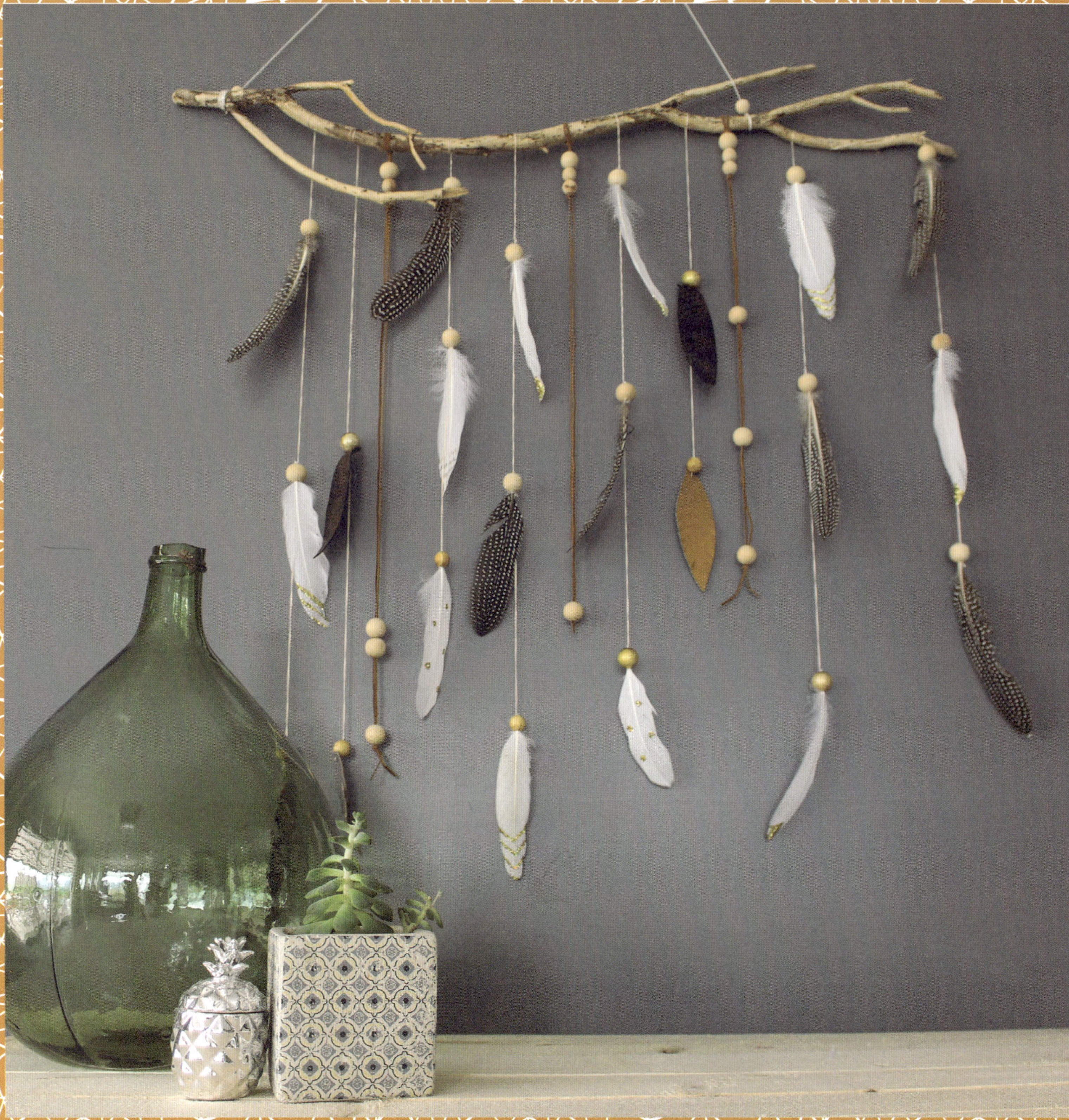

PRIMITIVE WALL HANGING

This is a spectacular wall hanging that combines natural feathers, textile feathers, and hand-glittered feathers. It will be perfect for hanging above the bed or the sofa.

LEVEL: 2 FEATHERS

Materials

- 1 nice branch of driftwood
- Remnants of leather and imitation leather
- Natural feathers in different colors
- Large white natural feathers
- Cotton thread
- Masking tape
- Several beads in different colors and textures
- Deer hide or leather cord
- 3-D textile paint
- Glitter glue
- Loose glitter
- Punch pliers
- Cutting pliers
- Dressmaker's scissors
- Hot glue gun
- Big-eye beading needle

1

Prepare the materials.

2. Cut small pieces of masking tape and place them on a feather according to the pattern you have chosen.

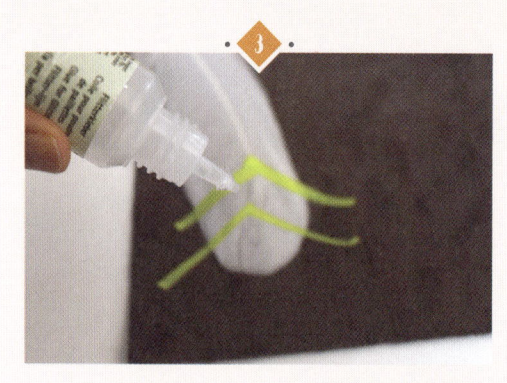

3. Put glitter glue on the areas not covered by the tape.

4. Dip the feather in a bowl of loose glitter and shake off the surplus.

5. Vary the shape of your pieces of masking tape to create different patterns.

6. Use the textile paint to add shapes or small dots on the feathers. Express your creativity!

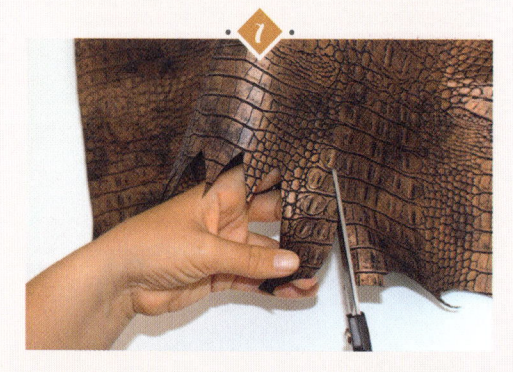

7. Cut out pretty feather shapes in the leather and imitation leather.

8. You can cut fringe in the feathers to give them more volume.

9. Use the punch pliers to make a hole in the end of your leather feathers to thread them onto the cotton thread.

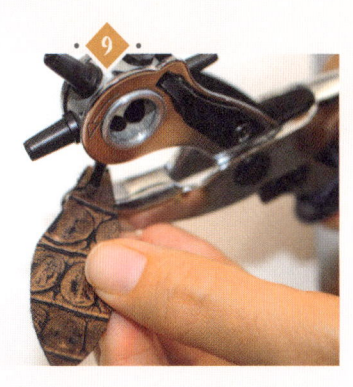

10. Wrap a length of cotton thread around one end of your driftwood branch and tie it firmly.

11. Thread beads all along the length of thread and tie the end tightly to the other end of the branch.

12. Cut different lengths of cotton thread and attach them to the driftwood, making a loop.

13. Do the same with the leather cords in different places on the branch.

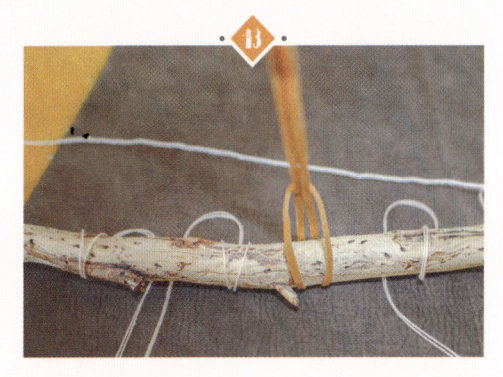

57

04. Thread wooden beads onto the leather cords. Place them however you like and make a knot at the end so that they don't slide off!

05. Use the bead needle to thread beads along your cotton threads. Slip feathers into the beads' holes, alternating natural feathers and decorated ones.

06. Put a drop of hot glue between the bead and the quill to attach them firmly together.

07. Slide the textile feathers along the cotton threads.

08. Cut the tips of the quills that are sticking out of the tops of the beads with the cutting pliers. Your wall hanging is finished!

× CHARLINE'S ADVICE ×

YOU CAN CUT SMALL FRINGES ON EACH FEATHER TO GIVE THEM MORE VOLUME. DON'T HESITATE TO MIX COLORS, TEXTURES, AND THICKNESSES OF CLOTH, LEATHER, AND HIDE TO GIVE YOUR CREATION A MORE AUTHENTIC LOOK.

Succulent Wall Hanging

This wall hanging is full of expression and freshness. These cute plants don't need any care, because your succulents are made of felt!

LEVEL: 3 FEATHERS

Materials

- Several branches of driftwood about 47 1/4 in. (120 cm) long
- Sheets of felt in shades of greens and grays
- Small white pebbles
- 3 transparent plastic open teardrops
- 2 transparent plastic open baubles
- Beads in different colors and textures
- Glass beads
- Unpolished wooden beads 1/2 in. (12 mm) diameter
- 5 mother-of-pearl beads
- Cotton thread
- Hemp cord
- Nylon thread
- 2 galvanized steel eye hooks 13/16 in. (30 mm)
- Dressmaker's scissors
- Cutting pliers
- Hot glue gun
- Bead needle
- Screwdriver

Prepare the materials.

2. Gather the branches of driftwood into a bundle and wrap the cotton thread around the center.

3. Tie a knot around the bundle and continue to wrap the thread around the branches.

4. Cover the cotton thread with hemp cord and add a drop of hot glue to secure it. The hemp cord will add a more natural feel.

5. Screw the eye hooks into one of the bundle's branches.

6. Cut 3 ft. 3 3/8 in. (1 m) of cotton thread.

7. Use the bead needle to thread 6 unpolished wooden beads onto the thread.

8. Put the white pebbles into the teardrops and baubles.

9. Add pretty colored beads to the middle of the pebbles.

10. Cut out 10 leaves around 2 in. (5 cm) long in the first sheet of felt and then 4 leaves in a different color.

11. Assemble these leaves to complement your arrangement.

12. Pinch the base of each leaf and apply a drop of hot glue to keep them folded, making petals.

13. Glue your felt petals together to shape your succulent. Pinch the petals between your fingers until the glue has set.

61

14. Glue a mother-of-pearl bead in the center of your succulent to give it an extra shine.

15. Repeat for the 4 other succulents. You can alternate the colors and vary the shapes and sizes!

16. Place the succulents into the teardrops and baubles that you have decorated with pebbles and beads.

17. Cut 5 lengths of nylon thread around 35 7/16 in. (90 cm) long. Thread glass or wooden beads onto the nylon.

18. Now tie your 5 suspensions at different lengths along the driftwood bundle.

19. You can also make this with fresh flowers for an ephemeral wall hanging that has even more punch!

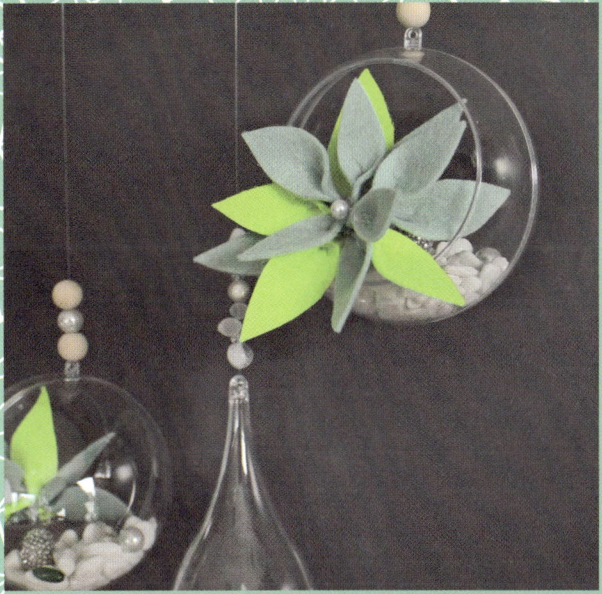

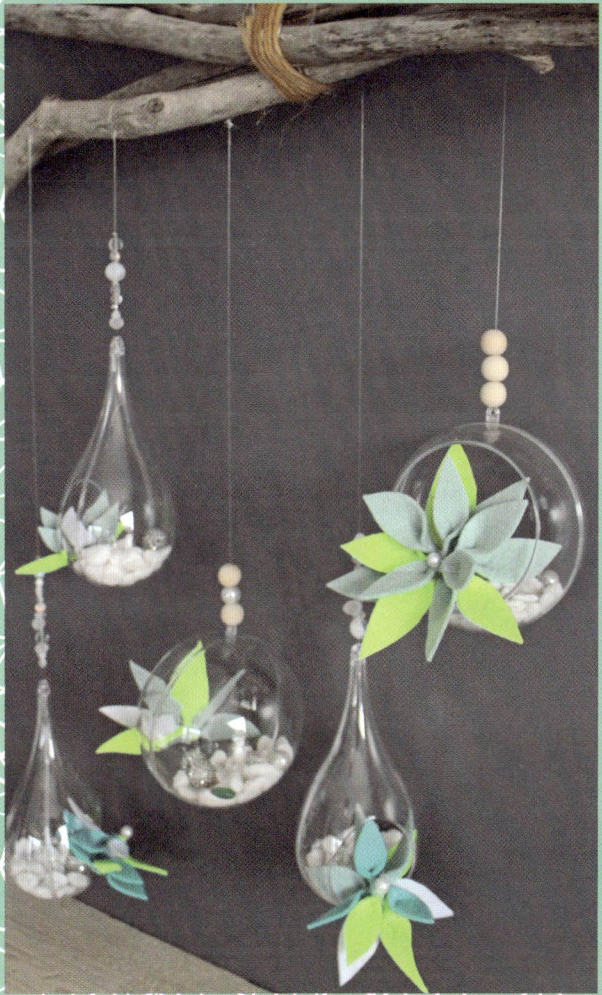

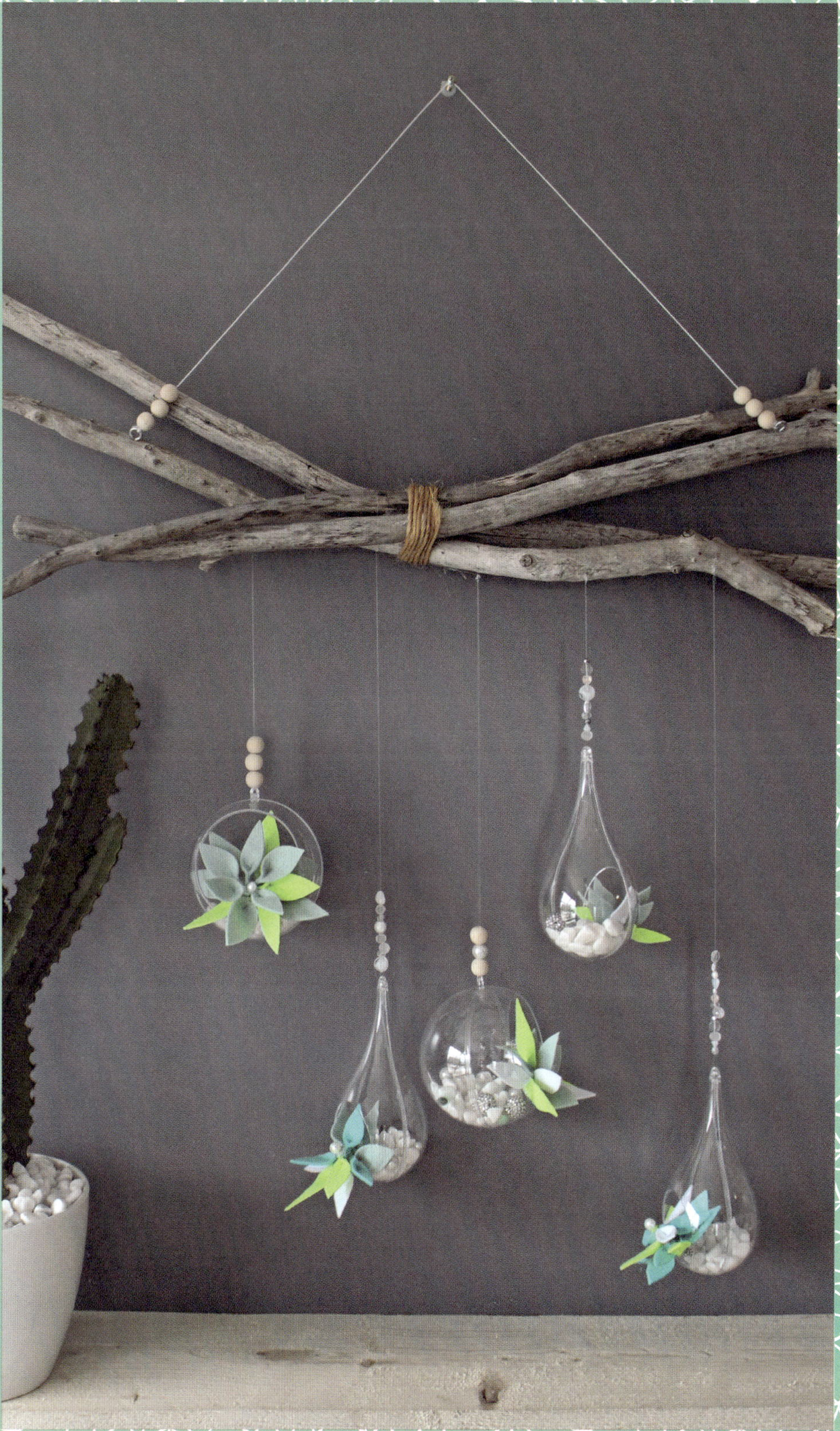

Materials

- Balls of yarn in different colors
- 3 branches of driftwood around 19 $^{11}/_{16}$ in. (50 cm) long
- Textile flowers
- Pom-pom maker (or a circle of cardboard with a hole in the center if you don't have this useful little gadget!)
- Wooden beads $^1/_2$ in. (12 mm) diameter
- Felt beads $^1/_2$ in. (12 mm) diameter
- 1 polystyrene bauble 3 $^{15}/_{16}$ in. (10 cm) diameter
- White satin ribbon $^1/_8$ in. (3 mm) wide
- Fishing twine
- Scissors
- Hot glue gun
- Drill
- 1 screw
- Big-eye beading needle
- 1 knitting needle (optional)

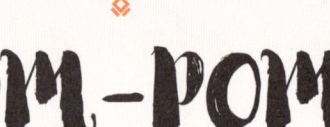

POM-POM MOBILE

A pretty, light, and colorful mobile for little children. Let yourself be swept away by the softness of wool pom-poms and go on a trip to the world of dreams!

LEVEL: 2 FEATHERS

Prepare the materials.

2. Make 4 big pom-poms and 8 little ones, changing the pom-pom maker (see the technique on page 19).

3. Now make pom-pom garlands: cut 4 lengths of fishing twine around 31 1/2 in. (80 cm) long and thread it onto your bead needle.

4. Pass the needle through the center of a big pom-pom to thread the twine through the pom-pom.

5. Then thread a wooden bead, a felt bead, and another wooden bead.

6. On the same twine, thread a small pom-pom followed by the beads. Repeat to obtain a garland with 3 pom-poms. Tie a knot in the end of the twine.

7. Keep the pom-poms and beads in place with a drop of hot glue.

8. Pierce the polystyrene bauble with the scissors or with a knitting needle.

9. Cut a length of twine around 19 11/16 in. (50 cm) and thread it through the bauble. Tie a knot in the end.

10. Glue your textile flowers to the bauble, leaving the twine visible.

11. Cross the 3 branches of driftwood on top of each other and drill through them. Screw them solidly together.

12. Tie the 3 pom-pom garlands to the driftwood branches with the fishing twine and add the flowery bauble in the center where the branches cross each other.

13. Cut 2 lengths of ribbon around 23 5/8 in. (60 cm) and tie each end to a branch to hang your mobile.

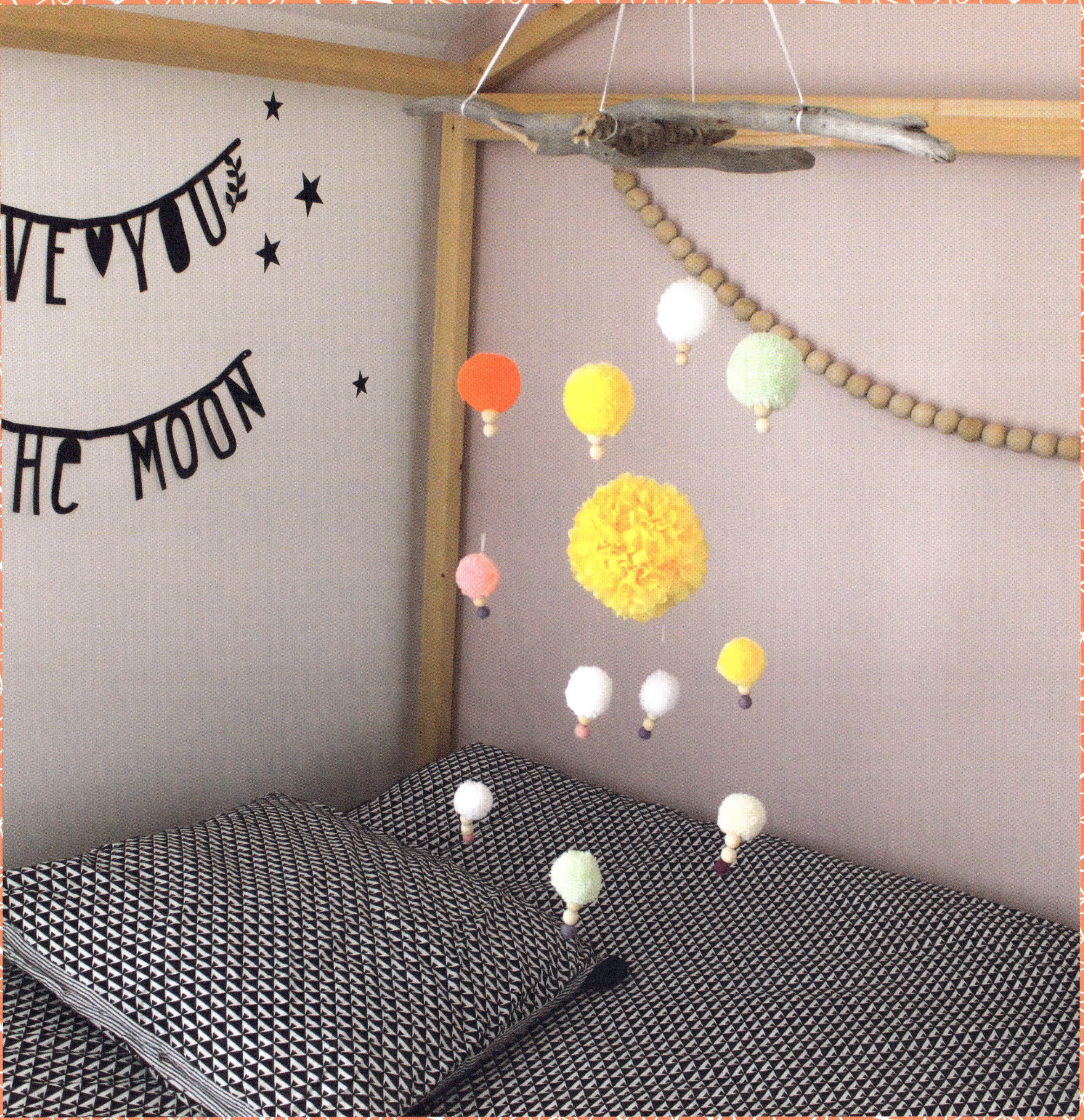
YOU
MOON

Materials

- 1 pair of Creole earrings 1 9/16 in. (40 mm)
- 2 earring hooks 11/16 in. (18 mm)
- Split rings
- 2 dream catcher pendants
- Several glass beads in different colors
- Several small cotton pom-poms
- Long-nose pliers
- Jewelry glue

Lucky Earrings

Delicate earrings made of glass beads and decorated with pretty cotton pom-poms, which will add charm to your summer or winter outfits. It is a simple project to follow, shown in two versions here. Give your imagination free rein—the possibilities are endless!

LEVEL: 1 FEATHER

Prepare the materials.

2. On each Creole, thread beads of your choice onto half of the earring.

3. Open a split ring with the pliers, insert it into the top of the pendant, and close it. Now thread the pendant onto the Creole.

4. Thread the rest of the beads onto the other half of the earring.

5. Add a little jewelry glue to the Creole's clasp and slip it into the small notch provided for this purpose.

6. Open the base of an earring hook with pliers.

7. Insert the small hook into the top of the Creole and close it.

69

Do the same with the little pom-poms: open the small hook with pliers, insert it into the pendant's small ring, and close it.

Repeat with the other two pom-poms. Your earrings are finished.

Add or change earring styles by inserting, for example, a little pom-pom into the center of the Creole.

70

Woven Necklace

A pretty necklace made of glass beads, resin beads, and delicate pom-poms makes for fashionable bohemian jewelry. A must for your summer outfits!

Materials

- Glass beads in different shapes and sizes
- Resin beads
- Split rings
- 1 dream catcher pendant
- 1 tassel maker
- Small cotton pom-poms
- White silk thread
- Long-nose pliers
- Jewelry glue
- Scissors
- Big-eye beading needle
- Cigarette lighter

LEVEL: 2 FEATHERS

Prepare the materials.

71

2. Choose the size of the tassel you want to make and position the silk thread in the notch provided for this purpose.

3. Wind the thread around the tassel maker about 20 times, according to the volume desired.

4. Now insert the thread into the second notch in the tassel maker.

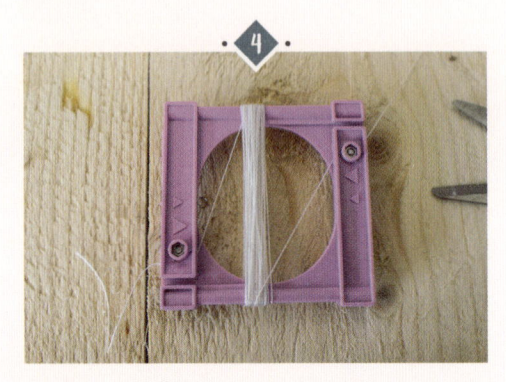

5. Cut a short length of thread and tie it tightly around the center of the bundle of threads on the machine.

6. Insert the scissors blade into the slot on the top of the tassel maker and cut through the threads. Repeat on the other side.

7. Fold the center knot in two and tie a short thread at the top. Make sure the length of the threads are equal to create a nice, even tassel.

Cut a length of around 19 $^{11}/_{16}$ in. (50 cm) of silk thread.

Pass it through the top of the tassel you have just made.

Insert the two strands into the bead needle. Thread on 7 glass beads, forming the base of your necklace.

Pass the silk thread through the dream catcher pendant. Tie a knot and add a little jewelry glue.

Thread a few beads onto the lengths of thread, tie a knot at each end, and snip off the surplus thread.

Cut 47 $^{1}/_{4}$ in. (120 cm) of silk thread, fold it in two, and slip it into the top of the dream catcher pendant. Tie a knot to keep the two strands in place.

Thread beads onto one of the strands. Be creative! Here, all the glass beads have been placed at the bottom of the necklace.

Finish with the resin beads to the end of the strand.

Repeat on the other strand, making sure the beads on the two strands match.

When you reach the end, tie the two stands together to join the necklace.

Add two small beads to the ends of the silk thread, and then burn the thread to finish your necklace.

Add small cotton pom-poms to the pendant using the split rings and the long-nose pliers.

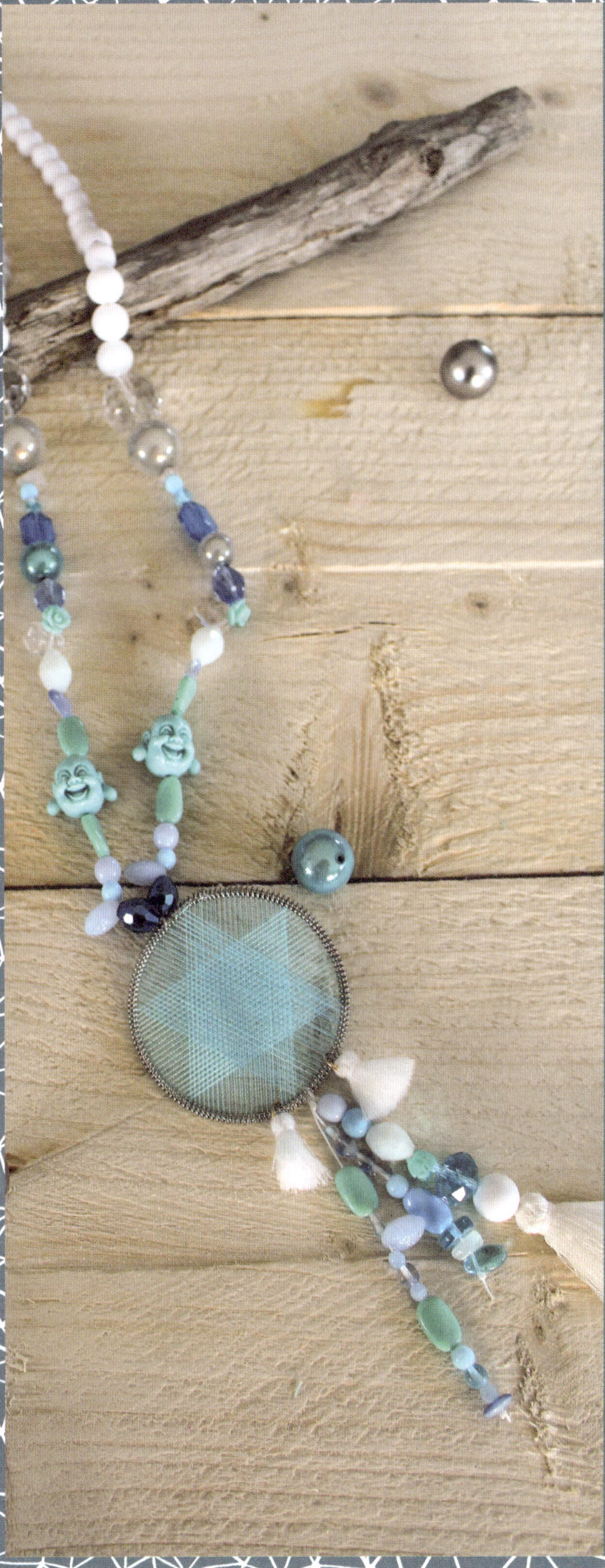
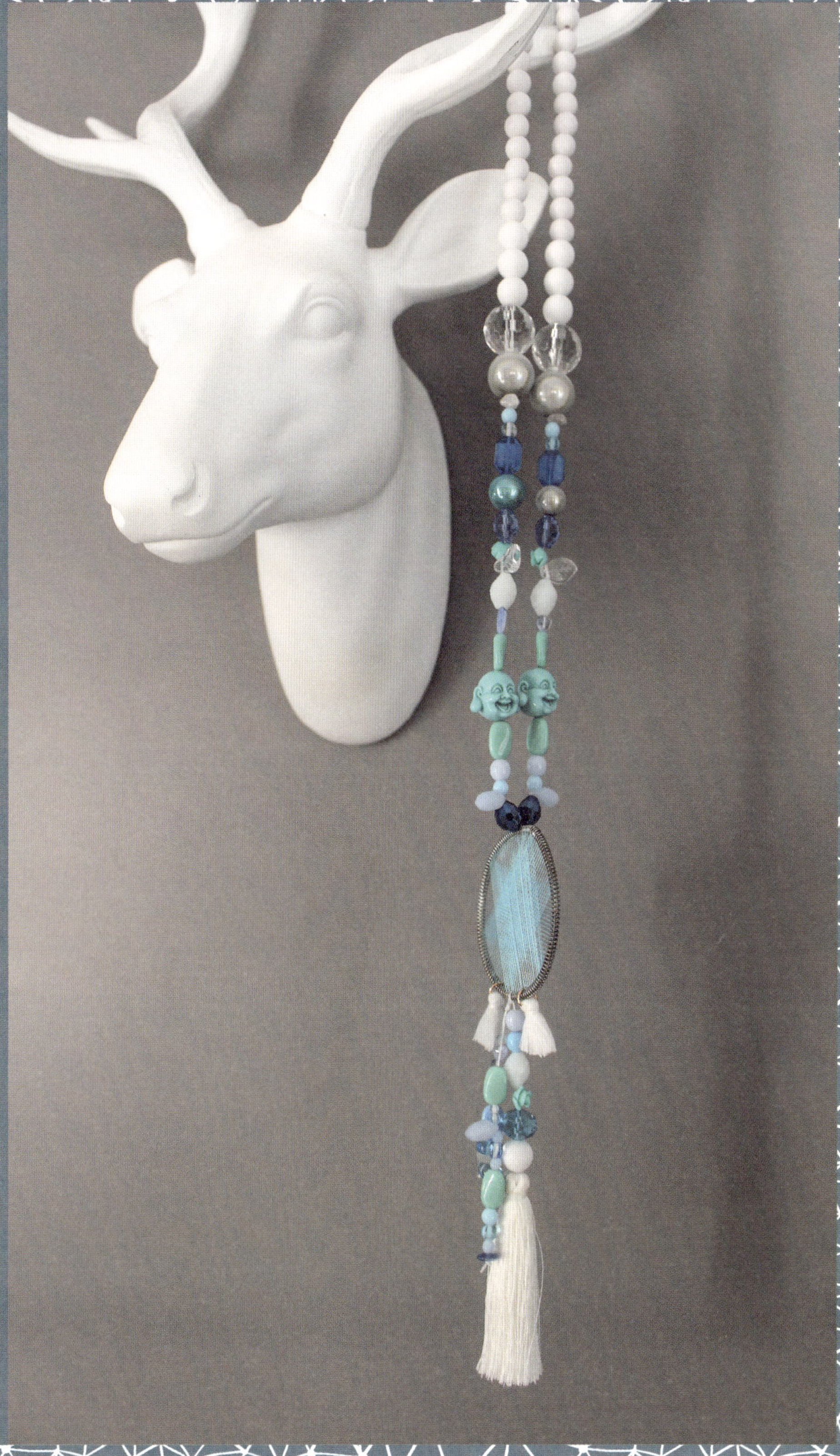

Materials

- 1 oval-link silver chain 35 7/16 in. (90 cm) long
- 1 dream catcher pendant
- Several glass beads
- 1 resin flower bead
- 1 small Swarovski rhinestone
- Tassel maker
- 3 split rings
- White silk thread
- Long-nose pliers
- Round-ended pliers
- Big-eye beading needle
- Jewelry glue
- Hot glue gun
- Scissors

Lucky Necklace

A delicate pendant necklace hung on a fine silver chain that will tastefully accent your outfits.

LEVEL: 1 FEATHER

Prepare the materials. Make the tassel (see page 72), which will become the pendant of your necklace.

· 2 ·

Use the gun to glue a small rhinestone onto the center of the dream catcher pendant and a small resin flower bead onto one side.

· 3 ·

Cut 19 ¹¹/₁₆ in. (50 cm) of silk thread and slip it into the bead needle. Pass it through the top of the tassel you made earlier.

· 4 ·

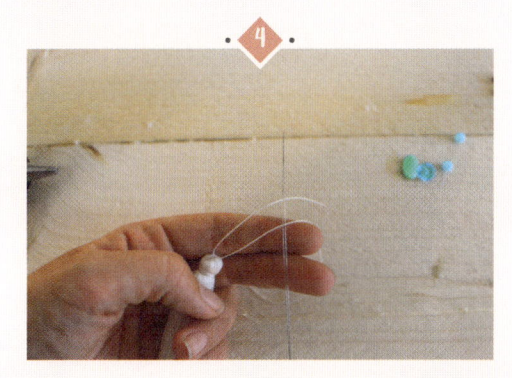

Center the thread and pass the ends through the bead needle.

· 5 ·

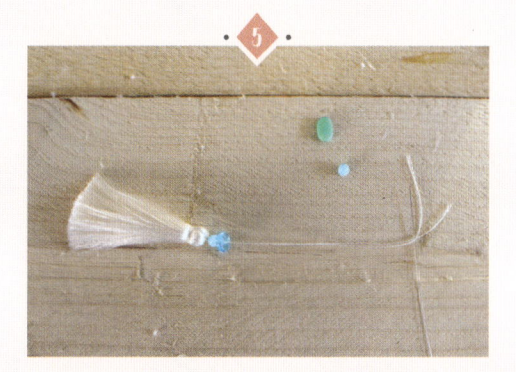

Thread 6 beads onto the strands to form the base of the necklace.

· 6 ·

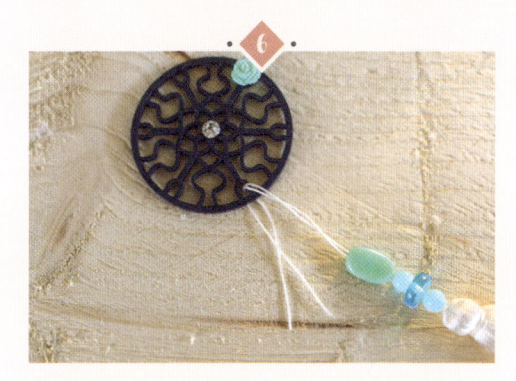

Thread the silk strands through the bottom of the pendant.

· 7 ·

Tie a knot and add a drop of jewelry glue.

77

· 8 ·

Using the round-ended pliers and the long-nose pliers, open a split ring.

· 9 ·

Place the ring at the top of the pendant and close it with the pliers.

· 10 ·

Pass the silver chain through the split ring.

· 11 ·

Open two more split rings and pass them through the last links on each end of the chain.

· 12 ·

Close one of the rings with the pliers. Slip the other ring into the first and close it with the pliers.

The author and the editor would like to thank the art stores *Matière Première* (www.matierepremiere.fr), *Créavéa*, (www.creavea.com), and *Perles & Co* (www.perlesandco.com), who supplied a large part of the materials, and notably *Perles & Co*, who supplied all of the materials for the models on pages 8–11, 12–16, 17–21, 30–35, 40–44, 45–49, and 64–67.

PERLES & CO
QUALITY AND CHOICE FOR CREATING ALL YOU DESIRE!

Find articles online at www.perlesandco.com

◆ JUNGLE DREAM CATCHER [PP. 8–11]
Driftwood branch: ref. PERS-156
Lizbeth cotton thread, size 20, 192 m, choice of colors: ref. FCU-23
Peacock feather, 25–30 cm: ref. CUSTO-236
Goose feather × 20 g, 15 cm, autumn: ref. CUSTO-675
Guineafowl feather × 10 g, 5 cm, natural: ref. CUSTO-673
Feathers × 10 g, 6 cm shades of green: ref. CUSTO-569
Round unpolished wooden beads × 10, 18 mm: ref. PB-188
Polished tagua nut, 35–50 mm, lime: ref. TAG-064
Green miracle beads × 20: ref. MAG-161
Light green/aniseed miracle beads × 20: ref. MAG-025
Green miracle bead 18 mm × 1: ref. MAG-133
Light green/aniseed miracle bead 18 mm × 1: ref. MAG-107
Round snakeskin bead, mustard, 20 mm: ref. PB-496
Grey tagua disc, 19 mm: ref. TAGU-051
Lime tagua disc, 19 mm: ref. TAGU-048
Brown glitter ribbon × 2 m, 10 mm: ref. FC-1084
Green glitter ribbon × 2 m, 10 mm: ref. FC-1073
Green satin ribbon × 5 m, 4 mm: ref. FC-550
Light olive satin ribbon × 5 m, 4 mm: ref. FC-549
Fine-tipped white Posca Marker, 1.3 mm: ref. OUT-248
Fine-tipped light green Posca Marker, 1.3 mm: ref. OUT-267
Fine-tipped light blue Posca Marker, 1.3 mm: ref. OUT-250

◆ BUFFALO DREAM CATCHER [PP. 12–16]
Cream-colored tulle: ref. TIS-639
Black feathers × 3 g 8–12 cm: ref. CUSTO-319
Round unpolished beads × 20, 8 mm: ref. PB-192
Resin rhinestone beads, 12 mm, choice of colors: ref. PLAS-026
Crystal Swarovski Hotfix rhinestones, 4 mm: ref. STR-133
Jet Swarovski Hotfix rhinestones, 4 mm: ref. STR-135
Light Colorado topaz Swarovski Hotfix rhinestones, 4 mm: ref. STR-115
Hotfix Artemio rhinestone applicator, 7 tips: ref. OUT-204
Hot glue gun: ref. OUT-414
Pom-pom maker kit: ref. LAINE-116

◆ ALL-WOOL DREAM CATCHER [PP. 17–21]
White lampshade hoop, 25 cm: ref. OUT-545
Lizbeth cotton thread, size 20, 192 m, choice of colors: ref. FCU-23
Resin rhinestone beads, 12 mm, choice of colors: ref. PLAS-026
Unpolished round wooden beads × 10, 18 mm: ref. PB-188

◆ PAPER FEATHER DREAM CATCHER [PP. 22–25]
Embroidery hoop, 20 cm: ref. TOOL-158
Lizbeth cotton thread, size 20, 192 m, choice of colors: ref. FCU-23
Turquoise miracle beads, 8 mm × 20: ref. MAG-027
Fuchsia miracle beads, 8 mm × 20: ref. MAG-033
Fuchsia miracle bead, 18 mm × 1: ref. MAG-104
Light turquoise miracle bead, 18 mm × 1: ref. MAG-131
Crocheted lace doily with heart pattern: ref. SEW-762

◆ AMERINDIAN DREAM CATCHER [PP. 30–35]
Piece of imitation leather, 50 × 30, choice of colors: ref. CUSTO-399
Tinted leaves of imitation Howlite, 22 m, multicolored: ref. SP-511
Punch pliers: ref. SEW-089
Lizbeth cotton thread, size 20, 192 m, choice of colors: ref. FCU-23
Bone beads × 35 g, multicolored: ref. ASS-157
Peacock feather, 25–30 cm: ref. CUSTO-236
Goose feather × 20 g, 15 cm, autumn: ref. CUSTO-675
Guineafowl feather × 10 g, 5 cm, natural: ref. CUSTO-673
Feathers × 10 g, 6 cm shades of green: ref. CUSTO-569
Round unpolished wooden beads × 10, 18 mm: ref. PB-188
Polished tagua nut, 35–50 mm, natural: ref. TAG-053
Light brown unpolished wooden heishi beads × 38 mm, 4 mm: ref. PB-687
Natural unpolished wooden heishi beads × 38 mm, 4 mm: ref. PB-688
Natural white açai seed beads, 10 mm × 10: ref. PB-652
Natural açai seed beads, 10 mm × 10: ref. PB-638
Swarovski mini-pear drop 6128, 12 mm, crystal pink gold: ref. WPF-1015
Loose silver or gold glitter: ref. TOOL-369

◆ SOPHISTICATED DREAM CATCHER [PP. 36–39]
White feathers × 100, 10–15 cm: ref. CUSTO-642
Lizbeth cotton thread, size 20, 192 m, choice of colors: ref. FCU-23
Swarovski rain drop 6022, 24 mm, crystal AB: ref. SWP-405
Round unpolished beads × 20, 8 mm: ref. PB-192
Crystal Swarovski Hotfix rhinestone, 4 mm: ref. STR-133

◆ TRIPLE-WEAVE DREAM CATCHER [PP. 40–44]
White metal hoop, 10 mm: ref. OUT-537
White metal hoop, 15 cm: ref. OUT-547
White metal hoop, 20 cm: ref. OUT-546
White metal hoop, 30 cm: ref. OUT-544
Lizbeth cotton thread, size 20, 192 m, choice of colors: ref. FCU-23
Round unpolished wooden beads, 18 mm: ref. PB-188
Driftwood branches, 2–9 cm: ref. PERS-025
White basic acrylic yarn: ref. LAINE-403
White feathers × 100, 10–15 cm: ref. CUSTO-642

◆ ROMANTIQUE WALL HANGING [PP. 45–49]
White crocheted lace doily pineapple, 29 cm: ref. SEW-806
Crocheted lace doily, heart pattern: ref. SEW-762
White crocheted lace doily, 25 cm: ref. SEW-761
Embroidery hoop, 11 cm: ref. TOOL-602
Embroidery hoop, 20 cm: ref. TOOL-158
Embroidery hoop, 30 cm: ref. TOOL-451

◆ MARINE WALL HANGING [PP. 50–53]
Driftwood branches, 2–9 cm: ref. PERS-025
Assortment mini-shells: ref. CSN-020
Puka shells, 2 holes: ref. CSN-024
Turquoise tagua nut: ref. TAGU-117
Lizbeth cotton thread, size 20, 192 m, choice of colors: ref. FCU-23
Braided nylon thread, 0.20 mm, crystal: ref. FC-457
Fine sand: ref. DECO-030

◆ PRIMITIVE WALL HANGING [PP. 54–58]
Camel suede effect leather cord, double stitching: ref. FILC-284

◆ POM-POM MOBILE [PP. 64–67]
Pom-pom maker kit: ref. LAINE-116
Round unpolished × 20, 8 mm: ref. PB-192
Mauve felt beads × 25, 10 mm: ref. FEUTRE-009
Natural felt beads × 25, 10 mm: ref. FEUTRE-010
Natural felt beads × 25, 20 mm: ref. LAINE-010
Polyester bauble, 80 mm: ref. ENF-205

◆ LUCKY EARRINGS [PP. 68–70]
Creoles × 2, 40 mm, silver: ref. BO-030

◆ LUCKY NECKLACE [PP. 76–79]
Crystal Swarovski Hotfix rhinestone, 4 mm: ref. STR-133

Copyright © 2019 by Schiffer Publishing, Ltd.

Originally published as *Attrape-Rêves* by Éditions Rustica, Paris © 2017.
Translated from the French by Omicron Language Solutions, LLC.

Library of Congress Control Number: 2018958778

All rights reserved. No part of this work may be reproduced or used in any form or by any means—graphic, electronic, or mechanical, including photocopying or information storage and retrieval systems—without written permission from the publisher.

The scanning, uploading, and distribution of this book or any part thereof via the Internet or any other means without the permission of the publisher is illegal and punishable by law. Please purchase only authorized editions and do not participate in or encourage the electronic piracy of copyrighted materials.

"Schiffer," "Schiffer Publishing, Ltd.," and the pen and inkwell logo are registered trademarks of Schiffer Publishing, Ltd.

Editing director: Elizabeth Pegeon
Editor: Juliette Magro
Copy preparation and proofreading: Melanie Le Neillon
Cover design by Caroline Soulères & Molly Shields
Production Design by Danielle Farmer

All photos by Charline Fabregues
Type set in Kinfolk Pro/DK Lemon Yellow Sun/Bear Hugs by Ratticsassin/Cervo Neue

ISBN: 978-0-7643-5738-1
Printed in China

Published by Schiffer Publishing, Ltd.
4880 Lower Valley Road
Atglen, PA 19310
Phone: (610) 593-1777; Fax: (610) 593-2002
E-mail: Info@schifferbooks.com
Web: www.schifferbooks.com

For our complete selection of fine books on this and related subjects, please visit our website at www.schifferbooks.com. You may also write for a free catalog.

Schiffer Publishing's titles are available at special discounts for bulk purchases for sales promotions or premiums. Special editions, including personalized covers, corporate imprints, and excerpts, can be created in large quantities for special needs. For more information, contact the publisher.

We are always looking for people to write books on new and related subjects. If you have an idea for a book, please contact us at proposals@schifferbooks.com.